Praise for *Dy*

"*Student engagement* has become such a dominant educational buzzword that it has almost become an educational end in itself, a learning outcome rather than what it really is: a learning process. *Dynamic Lecturing* could not come at a better time. It brings balance back to the pendulum by reminding us that student-centered activities should not be used to displace and replace the lecture, but to complement and augment it. This book meticulously documents how deep learning can and does occur when knowledgeable instructors share their knowledge with passion and enthusiasm, when they enliven academic content with meaningful personal stories, and when they model higher-level thinking skills for their students to emulate.

This book provides solid research-based evidence for the power of lectures and extensive evidence-based practices for magnifying their power. That being said, this book is much more than a book about lecturing. It demonstrates how lectures can be incorporated into an effective instructional sequence and seamlessly integrated with student questioning, student writing, small-group work, educational technology, and student assessment. *Dynamic Lecturing* is really a book about effective college teaching. It will make a valuable contribution to the professional development of current and future faculty."—***Joseph B. Cuseo****, Professor Emeritus, Psychology Educational Advisor, AVID for Higher Education*

"This book is a valuable resource for college professors and teachers for stimulating the engagement and learning of their students. Harrington and Zakrajsek have put together an array of lecture techniques and strategies (supported by evidence-based research), and as such, they demonstrate how we can use lectures as an effective teaching tool for moving our students to be more interested in their own learning. All in all, this book is an excellent resource for our learner-centered classrooms where lecturing and active learning are combined."
—***Kathleen Gabriel****, Associate Professor, School of Education, California State University, Chico*

"Finally, a book that lifts lecturing out of the land of ill-repute and positions it squarely in the midst of active learning strategies. Harrington and Zakrajsek present a plethora of simple strategies, based on numerous research studies, that will actively engage students in learning. This is a must-read for faculty who want to use lecturing as a tool to improve students' critical thinking and problem-solving skills."—***Saundra McGuire***,

(Ret.) Assistant Vice Chancellor; Professor of Chemistry; Director Emerita, Center for Academic Success, Louisiana State University

"This book is masterful in its ability to use modern research and thinking as a lens to inform an age-old method. As an advocate for inclusive teaching, it is wonderful to have a tool that honors this invaluable approach to instruction for both teachers and those they teach! I hope this book can help people who often use lecture as a last resort (like me) better embrace lecture for the powerful tool that it is."—***Carl S. Moore****, PhD, Assistant Chief Academic Officer, University of the District of Columbia*

"This book provides so many practical ways to apply neuroscience and cognitive psychology research in the classroom for more intentional teaching and better student outcomes. From developing lecture examples to carefully choosing your questions, this book reveals the specific adjustments in planning that will help to create the best learning environment for your students! I have already begun to incorporate many of these ideas into my classroom planning and my students are much more involved with the content! Fantastic book!"—***Kathy Nabours****, Associate Professor of Mathematics, Riverside City College*

"Headline news! Students can learn from lectures! This is Harrington and Zakrajsek's convincing, evidence-based argument. Their book is the first one on lecturing since Donald A. Bligh's (1998) fifth edition of *What's the Use of Lectures?* Academia really needs *Dynamic Lecturing*, especially because the lecture is still the most popular teaching method around. So let's stop trashing it and just do it well by 'accessorizing' it in some of the many low-effort ways Harrington and Zakrajsek recommend."—***Linda B. Nilson****, Director Emerita, Office of Teaching Effectiveness and Innovation, Clemson University*

"The authors of this book reorient and reintroduce readers to lecturing by providing best practices built upon the research regarding learning. Through this approach, *Dynamic Lecturing* dispels the false binary that often exists in active learning versus lecturing narratives. Whether you are new to teaching or are deep into your instructional career, you will find enormous benefits by reading this book."—***C. Edward Watson****, Associate Vice President, Association of American Colleges & Universities; and co-author of* Teaching Naked Techniques: A Practical Guide to Designing Better Classes

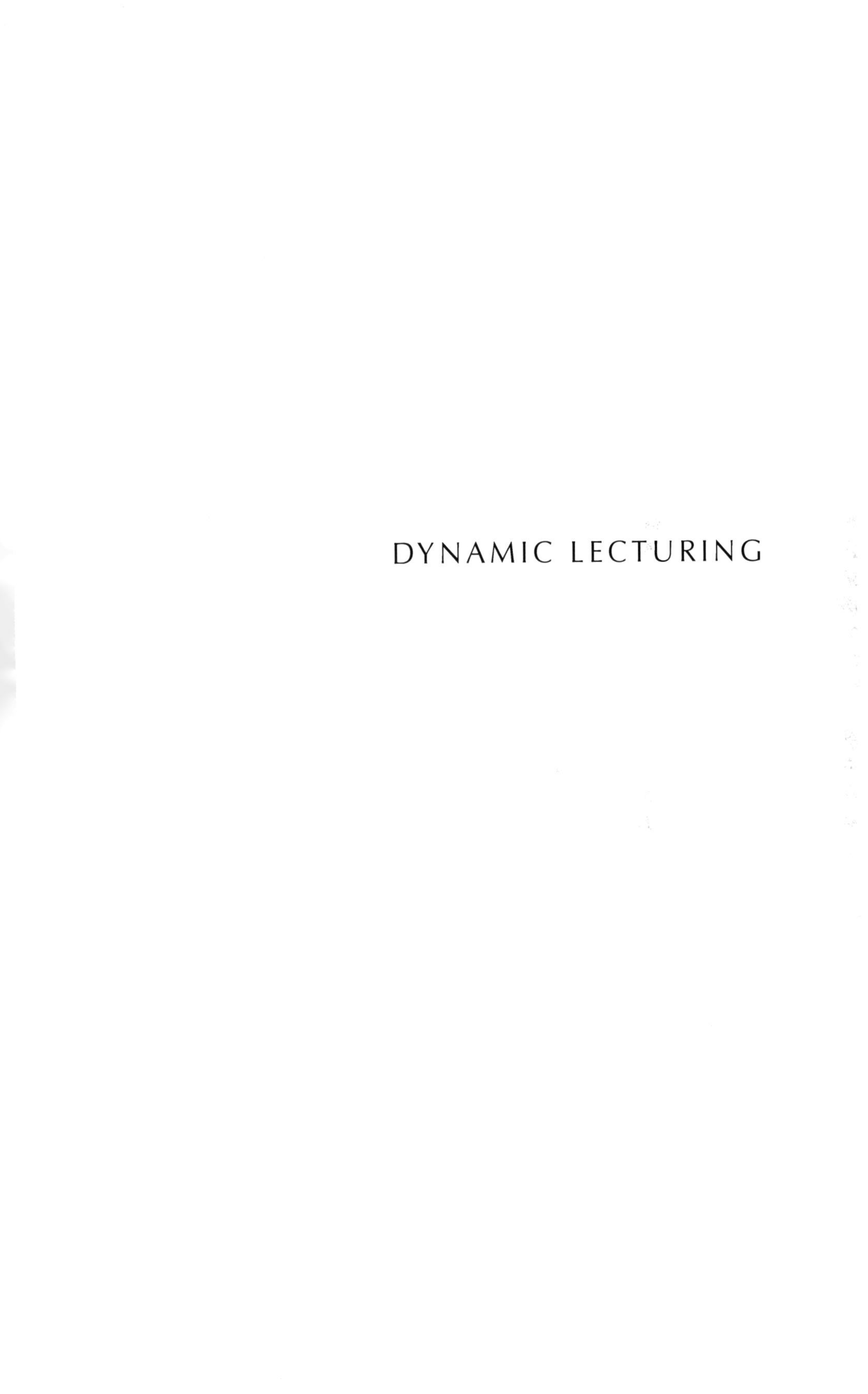

DYNAMIC LECTURING

The Excellent Teacher Series

Series Editor: Todd Zakrajsek

This series offers fresh approaches to teaching and learning by reviewing traditional methods in light of evidence-based strategies to promote practices that best facilitate student learning. Each volume of the series is written to provide early career faculty with specific strategies that can be quickly implemented, midcareer faculty with the opportunity to adapt and expand on what is currently used, and experienced faculty with new perspectives to augment thinking on foundational aspects of teaching and student learning. The following titles are forthcoming:

Understanding How We Learn: Applying Key Educational Psychology Concepts in the Classroom
By Todd Zakrajsek and Donna Bailey

The Syllabus as a Course Design Tool: Mapping a Learning Path for Your Students
By Christine Harrington and Melissa Thomas

Teaching Online: Creating Meaningful Learning in Digital Environments
By Kevin Kelly and Todd Zakrajsek

Off to a Great Start: Proven Strategies for Faculty Members New to Higher Education
By Todd Zakrajsek

DYNAMIC LECTURING

Research-Based Strategies to Enhance Lecture Effectiveness

Christine Harrington and Todd Zakrajsek

Foreword by José Antonio Bowen

Series Preface by Todd Zakrajsek

STERLING, VIRGINIA

Published by Stylus Publishing, LLC.
22883 Quicksilver Drive
Sterling, Virginia 20166-2102

Library of Congress Cataloging-in-Publication Data
Names: Harrington, Christine, 1971- author. | Zakrajsek, Todd, author.
Title: Dynamic lecturing : research-based strategies to enhance lecture effectiveness / Christine Harrington and Todd Zakrajsek.
Description: First edition. |
Sterling, Virginia : Stylus Publishing, 2017. |
Includes bibliographical references. | Description based on print version record and CIP data provided by publisher; resource not viewed.
Identifiers: LCCN 2016059965 (print) |
LCCN 2017026891 (ebook) |
ISBN 9781620366189 (Library networkable e-edition) |
ISBN 9781620366196 (Consumer e-edition) |
ISBN 9781620366165 (cloth : alk. paper) |
ISBN 9781620366172 (pbk. : alk. paper)
Subjects: LCSH: Lecture method in teaching. |
Teaching--Methodology.
Classification: LCC LB2393 (ebook) |
LCC LB2393 .H37 2017 (print) |
DDC 371.39/6--dc23
LC record available at https://lccn.loc.gov/2016059965

13-digit ISBN: 978-1-62036-616-5 (cloth)
13-digit ISBN: 978-1-62036-617-2 (paperback)
13-digit ISBN: 978-1-62036-618-9 (library networkable e-edition)
13-digit ISBN: 978-1-62036-619-6 (consumer e-edition)

Printed in the United States of America

All first editions printed on acid-free paper that meets the American National Standards Institute Z39-48 Standard.

First Edition, 2017

10 9 8 7 6 5 4 3

To Dan, Ryan, and David,
who keep me focused on what matters most.

—Christine

For Tim Sawyer,
who first taught me the power of the lecture.

—Todd

Contents

FOREWORD

What!? Me lecture? Not me. I must have wandered into the wrong book.

I began my academic career in the United Kingdom, where the entry-level job title is *lecturer,* and I was equally proud to earn the title of *professor* when I returned to America. Like most academics, I took these titles literally and spent the first half of my career honing ever more intricate lectures. Teaching music history initially required fumbling with stacks of records, then, later, cassette tapes of excerpts created for each class session. This curated collection of demo tapes was an organizational marvel, and I could easily collect my color-coded lecture notes and cassettes before each class. However, it had the perverse effect of etching my lectures in stone, since it was impossible to insert a new example in the middle of an existing cassette tape. The ability to burn a CD made it easier to revise and insert new musical examples from year to year, but it was the magical iPod that saved the day and finally allowed me to change direction in the middle of the hour and move to an unplanned musical excerpt when needed.

I made almost the same long pilgrimage with visual materials. I began with overhead projector films—I could write on them, in color! For pictures and images, there were slides, which had to be re-sorted after each lecture. And then God gave us the PowerPoint and I finally discarded the slides.

Now I could spend endless hours revising music examples, figures, text components, and images with my laptop as a central command station. I continued to print my extensive notes with their detailed instructions to play example number 15 while showing slide number 10 and then telling the joke about Beethoven's landlady.

I printed enormous course packs with dozens of pages of notes to accompany each lecture, and I made sure to include the names of all of the composers and musicians I might mention (with birth and death dates) as well as space for students to take their own notes at the appropriate time.

All of this without reading a single book on teaching!

Then, I discovered that there was, in fact, an entire scholarship of teaching and learning. Oops. So, I spent the next half of my career trying not only to not lecture but also to convince other people not to lecture. Converts make the best prophets. I inverted and then flipped my classroom, turned my old lectures into podcasts and videos, and created games. Finally, I decided I needed to go entirely naked (metaphorically) in every class, with pyramids of small group discussions, role playing activities, and all the active learning I could pack in.

You could, therefore, reasonably ask what I am doing here. Perhaps you are thinking that my conversion was not entirely pure, and that deep down I continue to pine for my role as the sage on the stage rather than the guide on the side? Or maybe you are hoping for that great American tradition of the public reversal? I got it all wrong and all of that research was a hoax!

I hate to disappoint you, but as Christine Harrington and Todd Zakrajsek have so clearly demonstrated, the answer to most good questions is, "It depends." This book solidly balances extensive research with useful summaries and practical advice. Most of us still lecture at least some of the time, and there are times when the lecture may still be the best use of your time with students. Lectures are indeed more effective when they are short and interspersed with active learning, but they can be especially important for novice learners. And lectures, like sermons, can be especially good at motivating, inspiring, and revealing your human side.

Practically, of course, most of us simply do not have the time, skill, expertise, and experience to redesign every course as a completely active learning experience. Even if we did, the first few times we teach that way, we are going to be learning ourselves. It is probably a much better strategy (and certainly one that is more likely to lead to work-life balance or a promotion) to add a few more of the active learning enhancements (as discussed in Part Two) and gradually improve the quality of your lectures.

This is an excellent and practical book. It will improve student learning in your classes, and that—without qualification—is what we all desire. If you are going to lecture anyway (and you are), you might as well get better at it. If you have limited time and too many students (and you do), then you could hardly ask for a more efficient and concise guide to making quick improvements that will make you a better teacher. Hallelujah that Christine and Todd have both the expertise and motivation to give us this wonderful new resource.

José Antonio Bowen
Goucher College

ACKNOWLEDGMENTS

Christine

There are so many influential people who have helped me grow personally and professionally. My parents; my husband Dan; my two sons, Ryan and David; my niece, Ashley; and my mother-in-law have always encouraged and supported me. I am also particularly grateful to my faculty and administrative colleagues at Middlesex County College for giving me the opportunity to serve as the director of the Center for Learning and Teaching and for sparking my passion for learning and teaching. I am also very appreciative of the faculty I meet at conferences such as the Lilly Conferences on College and University Teaching and Learning, which is where I met Todd Zakrajsek and John von Knorring from Stylus Publishing. Thank you, Todd and John, for believing in this book and for the amazing conversations we've had about lecturing and learning. Last, but certainly not least, I want to thank my students for inspiring me to more deeply explore teaching and learning processes.

Todd

I first and foremost thank my wife, Debra, to whom I turn whenever I have a fleeting idea to confirm it has merit and a potential place in the world. My children, Emma, MaryHelen, and Kathryn, must be acknowledged for providing me much to think about when it comes to teaching, learning, individual differences, and caring about others. All three are exceptional people. I wish to give a huge shout out to John von Knorring at Stylus Publishing for his keen understanding of higher education and insightful perspectives regarding the type of information that will enrich the professional lives of college and university faculty members. I learn from him every time we talk. Finally, I thank my students for their eagerness to learn, my colleagues for their willingness to share, and administrators for providing a place to play.

SERIES PREFACE

A primary challenge in higher education is rooted in an assumption that most of us faculty recognize all too well: If one has content knowledge, then the ability to effectively teach that information is a given. Essentially, it is assumed that with knowledge comes the ability to teach that knowledge to others.

This assumption is simply not valid, and for many of us hit home when we faced our first classroom full of learners. For more than 30 years I have watched this assumption—that knowledge comes automatically with the ability to teach—play out time and again, often in very subtle ways. I believe the assumption arises primarily from the fact that, in acquiring an advanced degree, content and research methods are carefully taught throughout the graduate program, while scant attention is given to the growing body of research findings that addresses how to teach any of that content to undergraduate students.

The good news is that a shift toward recognizing the need to develop teaching competence is occurring as graduate teaching seminars, workshops on teaching strategies specifically designed for graduate students, and better designed graduate teaching assistantships are becoming more and more prevalent. Unfortunately, many faculty members stepping into the classroom for the very first time have still received little, if any, pedagogical training. Additionally, there continues to be little effort to establish sufficient funding to help faculty maintain and enhance those strategies throughout their career as faculty members. How does it make sense that it takes more credentials to teach a 1st-grade class than it does either an undergraduate course or a graduate seminar?

The Excellent Teacher series is designed to address these issues. The topics and content are based on more than 20 years of my experience assisting faculty members with enhancing student learning through better teaching strategies. When working with faculty groups I often ask, "What do you find most difficult or challenging in creating effective learning environments for your students?" I have now collected and read literally thousands of responses to this question from faculty throughout the United States and abroad. The faculty responses to this question, along with over three decades of experience teaching in a variety of educational settings, have given me a solid understanding of what faculty struggle with and serve as the foundation for this series. For many titles, I have selected authors or coauthors who are recognized experts in the topic area and share my vision of what faculty are looking for to become better educators.

Our collective objective is to provide you with a strong introductory foundation to each topic. We have written these books with three specific goals in mind: to (a) write in accessible language for faculty in all disciplines and with varying levels of teaching experience, (b) provide you with evidence-based suggestions and strategies, and (c) provide sufficient background and data to give you the confidence to experiment. For example, the first book in the series, *Dynamic Lecturing: Research-Based Strategies to Enhance Lecture Effectiveness*, comes at a time when lecturing is being attacked as ineffective. The book argues that lecturing itself is not a bad teaching strategy, but rather that bad lecturing is. Research shows that lecturing can be extremely effective when paired with engaged learning strategies. The book provides the rationale and examples of strategies you can easily adopt.

The titles in this series are all self-contained. None presupposes reading of prior volumes. What connects them is a common feel and voice. Jump into whichever topic addresses an area you feel has most relevance to your concerns as a teacher or that appeals to your curiosity as you explore effective ways to engage your students and facilitate their learning of your disciplinary concepts. The concepts and strategies are applicable across all disciplines, as well as to all types of courses, from undergraduate to graduate levels, at all types of institution. The authors draw on workshops given with solid success at research extensive universities, comprehensive undergraduate institutions, private colleges, community and technical colleges, highly selective institutions, and those with open access. There are certainly many differences throughout higher education, but it turns out that there are also some striking similarities when it comes to providing good learning opportunities for our students. Those similarities are the themes for these volumes.

The Excellent Teacher series is the result of extensive work by exceptional educators who authored these books and the massive amount of research done by the talented individuals who completed the educational research so frequently cited. Our hope is that this series results in fresh approaches to teaching and learning by reviewing traditional methods in light of evidence-based strategies to promote practices that best facilitate student learning. Each volume of the series is written to provide early career faculty with specific strategies that can be quickly implemented, midcareer faculty with the opportunity to adapt and expand on what is currently used, and experienced faculty with new perspectives to augment thinking on foundational aspects of teaching and student learning.

Teaching is important beyond imagination, anything but easy, and provides us glimpses of the best of humanity, which is why I suspect we all engage in this noblest and challenging of professions. I do sincerely hope you find this series helpful and wish you well in your teaching endeavors.

Best,
Todd Zakrajsek

INTRODUCTION

DESPITE THE LECTURE BEING one of the most widely used teaching methods in higher education, few professional resources have been developed to guide faculty on how to use this teaching strategy effectively. The dearth of resource material on lecturing is likely because of beliefs that faculty should avoid lecturing and should instead rely primarily on more active learning approaches. Although increasing the use of active learning approaches has been shown to improve motivation and learning, research to date has not supported abandoning the lecture altogether. There are a variety of effective approaches to teaching, and the lecture is among those potentially effective approaches. Research and theory should always guide us in effectively implementing one's chosen teaching methods. As we all know, almost any teaching method will range from effective to ineffective based on the instructor, the students, and the content. Thus, it is critical for us to take a learning-centered approach to teaching and provide resources to help faculty effectively use all the major teaching methods.

This book was written to fill this need for research-based guidance on how to lecture effectively. After explaining why the lecture is still a valid teaching method, the focus of the book is on research-based strategies to understand when the lecturing technique is effective and how it can be enhanced by including engaged learning strategies. We hope you will walk away with a sense of validation, armed with research support for this tried-and-true teaching method. In addition, and perhaps more important, we hope you will also walk away with several new research-based strategies you can incorporate into your lectures. Finally, we hope that the lecture planning and evaluation tools provided will help you rework your lectures in ways that provide high-level engagement and achievement for your students.

This book is divided into three main parts. Part One (Chapters 1 and 2) is focused on the lecture as a legitimate teaching strategy and on the various types of lectures. In Chapter 1 we explore the benefits of the lecture. We review several research studies, highlighting the value of the lecture, especially for novice learners. In essence, this chapter provides evidence for lecturing, at least some of the time. Chapter 2 focuses on the different types of lectures. Overviews of formal paper-reading lectures, storytelling lectures, discussion-based lectures, visually enhanced lectures, demonstration lectures, online lectures, and interactive lectures are provided along with the advantages and disadvantages of each method.

Part Two (Chapters 3–9) focuses on the following educational strategies to enhance the lecture: activating prior knowledge, capturing attention and emphasizing important points, effectively using multimedia and technology, making concepts meaningful through examples, including reflection opportunities, demonstrating the importance of retrieval practice, and using questions to promote critical thinking. Each chapter includes a discussion of the strategy, the educational theory pertaining to that strategy, and research support. The focus of each chapter then shifts to practical applications with numerous suggestions about how to improve learning by incorporating engagement techniques into the lectures that align with the educational strategies presented in the chapter.

Part Three (Chapters 10 and 11) is devoted to helping faculty effectively plan for lecturing and helping chairs, administrators, or peers effectively evaluate the lecture. We hope you find the tools and resources useful, such as the planning and evaluating forms provided in Chapter 10 and Chapter 11, as you develop and evaluate lectures. The end goal is, of course, improved student learning.

PART ONE

EXPLORING THE LECTURE

1

THE LECTURE AS A TEACHING STRATEGY

For more than 900 years, lectures have been the primary strategy for teaching in higher education, dating from the start of universities in Western Europe (Brockliss, 1996). Over the past 25 years, however, many have argued that faculty members need to abandon the lecture and shift to more active learning approaches (Bajak, 2014; Bligh, 2000; Freeman et al., 2014; Hakeem, 2001). One prominent push to remove lectures was King's (1993) often cited proposition for higher education faculty members to move from being *the sage on the stage to the guide on the side*. The premise behind this widely known phrase is that lecturing is not an effective teaching approach because students are not actively engaged when listening to a lecture. This position is based on constructivist theories that focus on students benefitting from being active participants and coconstructors of knowledge rather than empty vessels that need to be filled with knowledge. The implication of this argument is that the lecture is simply a one-directional transmission of knowledge from expert to student, with students in a passive role waiting to simply receive the information from the professor.

Around the same time that King (1993) discussed the importance of moving toward being a wise facilitator in an active classroom, Barr and Tagg (1995) called for a similar paradigm shift in education, arguing that learning rather than teaching should be the focus in higher education. This call to action asked faculty to change from a teacher-centered approach to a student-centered approach to learning. In essence, faculty members were encouraged to think about learning first and teaching second. Because many viewed the lecture as teacher focused and active learning as student focused, faculty members were encouraged to move from lecturing to more active and engaged learning approaches. As a result, conferences and books devoted to pedagogical approaches moved en masse to active learning themes. An extensive systematic review of traditional lecturing versus active learning concluded that "calls to increase the number of students receiving STEM degrees could be answered, at least in part, by abandoning traditional lecture in favor of active learning" (Freeman et al., 2014, p. 8410). With all the research and focus on active and engaged learning designed to replace lectures, teaching and learning centers across the nation followed suit, supporting faculty members in their use of active learning approaches, such as small-group work, to engage all students and set the stage for learning.

Unfortunately, many have interpreted the move to active learning to mean that the lecture should be abandoned. The call to include more active strategies and the push to emphasize more learner-centered instruction was not based on evidence that lecturing was in itself a bad instructional approach. Research noted that traditional lectures used alone were ineffective, but that lectures mixed with active learning were found to be an effective teaching strategy (Freeman et al., 2014). Lectures can have very powerful effects. It is actually very easy to demonstrate the strong potential of the lecture to teach an individual who is a novice in any field. Imagine for a moment that you wish to teach a novice which combination of chemicals will explode. Telling a student that the following information will affect his or her life and then describing the chemicals that will explode when mixed will certainly lead to new knowledge. In this example, active learning would potentially be the worst teaching strategy. The same case could be made in any number of disciplines when providing foundational knowledge that allows critical and creative thinking to follow. The lecture can be even more powerful when combined with active learning techniques. The evidence that drove many faculty members to move from lecture to active learning actually demonstrated that incorporating reflection and engaged strategies into the lecture format enhances long-term recall of newly acquired information (Hake, 1998). Unfortunately, the call to move from lecture to active learning is often interpreted as an either-or proposition and pitted active learning against the lecture. This has led to individuals suggesting that active learning approaches should fully replace the lecture or that the lecture should be banned altogether (e.g., Bajak, 2014). As a result, some have discouraged faculty members from lecturing, and some question whether it is even ethical to lecture (Handelsman, 2011). This is quite unfortunate, as the lecture can be an extremely effective teaching strategy. As Stacy (2009) noted, “Lecturing, like most things, can be done well and can be done badly” (p. 275).

Everyone seems to agree that boring, monotone, ineffective lectures do exist. That said, completely abandoning a teaching strategy that has been around for nearly a century based on the poor implementation of that strategy by some is certainly not productive. Regmi (2012) points out that boring lectures are the result of the instructor’s lack of skills, not the teaching method itself. To enhance learning, it is important to carefully evaluate all the available effective teaching methods and assist faculty with implementing each of those teaching methods effectively.

The lecture is most certainly on the list of teaching methods that can be effective. Most would agree that lectures provided via TED talks (www.ted.com/talks) are well done and effective. This is not to say that one should lecture all the time; rather, a combination of teaching approaches will likely work best. Research has shown that professional development aimed at improving the lecture by incorporating interactive strategies is effective (Nasmith & Steinert, 2001). Snowball (2014) found that adding online activities to a traditional lecture was an effective way to “improve teaching and learning and to accommodate student diversity” (p. 823).

Even with the massive push in higher education to move away from the lecture to more active learning methodologies, lecturing is still the most widely used teaching method (Berrett, 2012). Unfortunately, very few professional development resources focus on helping faculty to lecture effectively. It is difficult, if not impossible, to find sessions at higher education teaching and learning conferences that address how to lecture well. Books on the topic of effective lecturing are scarce. Likewise, many teaching and learning centers do not provide workshops or other support for faculty who lecture. In fact, some centers completely avoid supporting lecturing in any way, as it may present an image that is inconsistent with their mission of creating engaged learning environments.

Despite the lack of pedagogical support, the lecture is an effective teaching strategy when done well, particularly when combined with active learning techniques. The critical factor is to look at what constitutes an effective lecture, the types of lectures, and how to best determine when and what type of activities to combine with a lecture.

LECTURING WORKS: A LOOK AT THE EVIDENCE

If done well, the lecture may produce some of the highest levels of learning (Baeten, Dochy, & Struyven, 2013; Clark, Kirshner, & Sweller, 2012). Klahr and Nigam (2004) conducted an experimental study to investigate the effectiveness of the lecture approach. In their study, 112 third and fourth grade students were randomly assigned to direct instruction or discovery-based learning, which is a learning environment where students work together to discover content. Results of this study revealed that students in direct instruction greatly outperformed the students in the discovery-based learning section. Specifically, 77% of the children in direct instruction mastered the content as they were able to complete three of four tasks successfully. Only 23% of the children who participated in the discovery-based learning process mastered the content. In another study, Baeten and colleagues (2013) also found the lecture method beneficial. In this quasi-experimental study, college classes were taught using one of the following methods:

- lecture only,
- case-based learning only,
- an alternating approach (lecture, case-based, lecture, case-based), or
- a gradual approach (lecture, lecture, case-based, case-based).

The case-based learning approach used a constructivist approach that actively involved the students; the teacher was in the facilitator role, and authentic assignments and group work were used. The researchers noted the students who were in a lecturing only or gradual approach class outperformed the students who were assigned to the case-based learning approach. Interestingly, students in the gradual approach group outperformed students in the alternating approach group. The students in the gradual approach learned by lecture during the first half of the semester and then participated in case-based learning during the second half of the semester. In the alternating approach, students first listened to a lecture and then participated in a case-based learning activity followed by another lecture and then another case-based learning activity. These findings suggest that lecturing is particularly important and useful early in a course, as lectures build foundational knowledge needed for active learning.

Research has found that the benefits of direct instruction may extend into the multimedia arena as well. In a study by Jensen (2011), students in an introductory psychology course received in-person and online lectures for different course content. No significant differences were found between online or in-person lecture formats. In other words, students performed equally well on quizzes regardless of whether the lecture took place in the classroom or online. However, it should be noted that students indicated it was easier to attend to the content when attending an in-person lecture as compared to the online lecture (Jensen, 2011). Toto and Booth (2008) found that access to online mini lectures increased test performance, suggesting that the value of listening to a lecture extends beyond the traditional, in-person lecture. One advantage of posting lectures online is that students can access the material as often as needed. This can be particularly helpful for students with learning disabilities who may benefit from listening to the lecture more than once. Although these findings support the use of online lectures, it is important to note that some researchers have failed to find positive effects of providing online lectures (Evans, 2014; Joordens, Grinnell, & Chrysostomou, 2009).

LECTURES ARE EFFICIENT AND EFFECTIVE FOR NOVICE LEARNERS

One of the main reasons lecturing continues to be so prevalent is that it is a very efficient teaching method. Given the large amounts of content and the limited amount of time in courses, at times efficiency is important. Although group work done well is certainly effective (Springer, Stanne, & Donovan, 1999), much more instructional time is needed for this teaching method. Unfortunately, the amount of time undergraduates spend in class is quite limited, and professors need to carefully consider the best use of precious instructional time. College students are expected to learn a vast amount of content, particularly when being introduced to a new subject area. The lecture teaching method, compared to group or other active learning approaches, allows for more efficient learning of content. This is particularly important for courses with learning outcomes that focus significantly on foundational knowledge. One solution is to skillfully share content via a lecture and then augment it with interspersed brief interactive exercises. Lectures also ensure that the content is communicated accurately, which is particularly important in the early formation of a subject matter area. Although discovery-based learning can bring about tremendous long-term effects, one of the noted disadvantages of discovery-based learning is that students often require a significant amount of time and expend significant mental effort learning inaccurate or incorrect information (Kirschner, Sweller, & Clark, 2006). When this happens, additional time must be spent on helping students unlearn the inaccurate content and learn the accurate content, a task that is not only time consuming but also quite challenging. Overall, the lecture mixed with active learning strategies brings about a compromise of efficiency and deep learning.

Lecturing is efficient because it reduces the cognitive load for students (Lee & Anderson, 2013). In other words, it is easier and less taxing for students to hear you, the expert, explain a concept rather than work with others, who often do not know much about the concept, to try to understand it on their own. Research conducted by Tuovinen and Sweller (1999) nicely illustrates this concept. In their study, students were assigned to either a worked example or an exploration group. Worked examples are when a faculty member demonstrates an example during a lecture, such as a math professor who works out the problem in front of the class, showing students the process behind obtaining the correct answer. Exploration groups seek to figure out the correct answer without seeing an example problem worked out. In addition to measuring success, Tuovinen and Sweller also assessed cognitive load and task efficiency. They found that for students who had little to no background knowledge, the worked example learning method was much more efficient than the exploration method. In other words, the more direct, worked example approach did not demand as much mental energy for new learners and resulted in significantly more learning.

A large part of learning is learning how to think about the subject or problem at hand. In such cases, watching an expert think through the solution is beneficial. This is the basis of social learning: We learn from watching others. With respect to the lecture method, the expertise of the professor is critical to the learning process. Think about how an expert can effectively organize information for students, explicitly make connections between concepts, and emphasize the concepts or theories that are most important. Research has shown that these tasks are quite difficult for novice learners who are not able to easily differentiate the important from the less important or identify the connections between concepts (Hrepic, Zollman, & Rebello, 2007). Students gain a lot from watching professors use their expertise to solve problems. In other words, students learn from observing the process used in talking about the subject as well as the content itself. In a study by Jensen (2011), students reported that in-person lectures were most helpful in terms of understanding course content (88% agreed or strongly agreed that lectures helped them learn the course content) compared to active learning sessions (49% agreed or strongly agreed that these sessions helped them learn the course content). Students with little to no background on a subject find that the lecture helps them develop a strong foundational knowledge base in a much more time-efficient way than if they were left on their own to discover the connections and learn the content.

Because teaching and learning are such complex processes, it is important to consider the primary factors that might help us decide when it is best to lecture and when it is best to use more active learning approaches.

One important factor that we have not yet addressed is the student's background knowledge on the subject matter. Research has found that lecturing (i.e., direct instruction) is most helpful to individuals with limited knowledge in a given area (Clark et al., 2012). In other words, students who do not have much background in a content area will learn best when an expert shares knowledge about the topic in a lecture. This may explain why Baeten and colleagues (2013) found that the gradual approach (lecture during the first half of the semester followed by case-based small-group work during the second half) worked better than the alternating approach (lecture, case-based learning, lecture, case-based learning). Lecturing can provide students with the background knowledge they need to be successful in group work or other active learning experiences. Faculty have spent a great deal of time developing expertise in areas where students hope to learn. When asked to engage in group work without adequate background knowledge, students often get frustrated, focus on nonessential details rather than the most important concepts, and may spend their time and energy on learning inaccurate information (Kirschner et al., 2006; Woolfolk, 2013). This is because students do not yet know enough about the discipline to productively contribute and participate in constructing knowledge through group work. Background knowledge is an essential factor for engaging in higher level thinking (Harrington, 2016).

With respect to acquisition of information through lecture and active learning, experts differ from novices. Lee and Anderson (2013) describe the expertise reversal effect, with experts benefitting more from active group work than from lecturing. With advanced undergraduate or graduate students, it is better to increase the amount of active learning strategies and decrease time spent lecturing, as these students will likely learn best in a learning environment that focuses on in depth discussions and group activities. This shifting in benefits of strategies occurs as more advanced students have more background information in the area being studied. The main point is that the effectiveness of lectures and active learning differs by level of expertise. Novice learners, those with limited background knowledge in a given area, will benefit more from a higher proportion of lectures than they would from a higher proportion of active learning, whereas the reverse is true for more advanced learners. This doesn't mean that group work and other active learning approaches should be avoided. Research clearly shows that some form of active learning strategy will help novice learners solidify the information just learned. However, a measured amount of lecturing is particularly beneficial to the novice learner. As a faculty member, it is important to consider what background knowledge students need to be successful in the group activity and then be sure that students have an opportunity to learn this necessary background knowledge before letting them work in groups. In other words, lectures should typically precede group work in undergraduate education, especially in courses that do not have prerequisites. As students gain more background knowledge in a subject area, the teaching methods can shift, and active learning can become the primary learning method. This suggests that lecturing may well be more beneficial in first- and second-year classes, whereas small-group discussions and activities more appropriately dominate the graduate student classroom. This research illustrates the importance of knowing your students. All teaching approaches are not equally effective with all students, and no strategy should be used in isolation. To repeat, background knowledge is one important consideration when determining which teaching method to use.

THE POWER OF A GOOD STORY

Although lectures have a variety of forms, one very effective component of the lecture is telling a story to illustrate the content and the critical thinking process of a discipline. As noted by Cangelosi and Whitt (2006), "Storytelling is a long standing method of teaching that has been effective in a wide variety of formal and informal learning environments" (p. 1). A good story is an incredibly powerful learning tool, and humans have been using the power of stories effectively for centuries. Well-developed storytelling captures and maintains the attention of students (Lordly, 2007) in part because of the emotional aspect of stories. It also puts information into a framework that is easier to understand and to process. Essentially, it is easier to connect to content when we can easily relate to it. Emotions provide a vehicle for this connection even when our experiences with the content may be limited. According to social neuroscientists, emotional contagion occurs in humans. Emotional contagion is one factor pertaining to emotion and learning that has been shown to have an impact on task performance and cooperation (Barsade, 2016). Emotional contagion occurs when a person's mood is influenced by the mood of other individuals. Being positive results in others becoming more positive by association. In essence, the way in which content is delivered matters. In other words, as social animals, our emotions can draw in other individuals as they relate to our emotions, making it more likely for students to attach more personal value to the content. Not surprisingly, emotions play a huge role in learning. When a lecturer shares her/his passion with students, this emotional experience motivates and inspires. Students are more likely to learn from a professor who is passionate than from one who does not exude excitement and passion about the discipline. In fact, one of the primary reasons cited for ineffective lectures is a lack of emotion in the lecturer's delivery, such as reading text or explaining a concept in a monotone voice. Physiological mechanisms at play make it difficult for a person to listen to emotionless information. Effective storytellers skillfully organize the content, often but not always sequentially, and interweave details and emotion to make the content come alive.

In the discussion of active versus passive learning, some argue that lecturing is passive because the listener simply sits there and receives information as an empty vessel into which knowledge is being poured. A good story can result in a very actively engaged listener. Mayer (2009) argues that the most important type of engagement in learning is cognitive engagement, and high cognitive engagement is likely to occur during a good story. Think about how listeners can be incredibly engaged, sometimes even sitting on the edge of their seat, when listening to a story or captivating lecture. Although students in this situation may not be talking with others or working in a hands-on way, students can most certainly be engaged from a cognitive standpoint. If cognitive engagement is what matters most, then stories delivered by lecture can be an incredibly powerful teaching method.

Stories also give meaning to the content being learned. Putting information in a meaningful context significantly increases learning. Story lines have a beginning, a middle, and an end, and this overall organizational structure and resolution makes it easier for students to take in and digest the information. Using short stories within the context of a larger story also helps individuals to better understand complicated concepts and situations. In other words, faculty can organize or structure their lecture according to an overarching theme or story line but then venture out by telling short stories that relate to more specific content. Mini stories that elaborate on content and give additional meaning to the material being learned will undoubtedly increase learning. Examples in the form of mini stories help the students make sense of the content and bring the information alive (Lee & Anderson, 2013). Relational elaboration, comparing and contrasting elements within a given area of content, is a particularly effective strategy. By focusing on similarities and differences, learning can be significantly increased (Hamilton, 1997). Although relational elaboration naturally happens when using the storytelling approach, Eagan (1982) argues that teachers can plan to use binary opposites such as good versus bad to create a structure that results in higher levels of student understanding and engagement.

Relatedly, professors often incorporate metaphors into lectures, especially when introducing new concepts or perspectives (Beger, 2011). Metaphors, which typically allow an established concept to be applied to a concept being learned, can be used to provide an overall framework or context for new content and to also make the content more memorable. However, Littlemore (2001) notes that metaphors can have a negative impact on the learning process for students from different cultures or for those whose first language is not English. For example, it is common for students from different cultures or countries to misinterpret metaphors and the related course content. This can also be true for students with learning challenges. Students with high-functioning autism, for instance, often interpret language very literally and could therefore struggle with making sense of course content presented through metaphors (Gold & Faust, 2010). Thus, as faculty we need to be mindful of how metaphors might enhance or inhibit the learning processes for our students. When they work, metaphors are a powerful way to help students understand abstract or complex concepts. At times, however, the use of metaphors may lead to students walking away with inaccurate understandings of the material. Communicating content in several different ways and explaining metaphors in detail can potentially help combat some of the possible pitfalls with this teaching approach.

It should be noted that storytelling works well for novices and experts, as even those with a great depth of information in a given area love a good story. Faculty often pour into professional development sessions conducted by prestigious members of their discipline to hear them share their stories in a lecture. Although many of us do appreciate conferences and other professional development opportunities that allow interaction and reflection, we also love a well-crafted lecture, provided it is developed and delivered well. This explains the popularity of TED talks, which are a perfect example of how lectures can be turned into powerful stories and how lectures can still be effective even with experts as audience members.

A BETTER APPROACH

Research to date on effective teaching and learning does not suggest we choose between lectures and active learning approaches. Instead, it is important to determine which learning approaches work best for which students under which learning conditions and by which instructor. Effective teaching is a complex process that involves the teacher, the student, the content, and the pedagogical approach (Pashler, McDaniel, Rohrer, &

Bjork, 2008). For example, if the learning outcome is for students to be able to use a microscope, then your teaching method should most definitely include a hands-on opportunity for students to learn and practice this skill. In this example, a lecture might be helpful prior to the hands-on activity to identify behaviors that might break the microscope or damage the slide being observed, but relying exclusively on the lecture method would be obviously problematic. If the course learning outcomes are focused on developing teamwork and collaboration skills, it will be difficult to achieve these outcomes by relying solely on the lecture teaching method. Clearly, students will need an opportunity to engage in group work to successfully achieve these learning outcomes.

The best approach to teaching is a blended one that incorporates lecture and active learning opportunities (e.g., Freeman et al., 2014; Major, Harris, & Zakrajsek, 2016). In addition, the passion you bring to your lectures can be an incredibly important factor in whether students learn and involve themselves further with the discipline. Skillfully integrating active learning strategies into a well-crafted lecture can have amazing outcomes. For example, adding brief opportunities for students to digest and reflect on the content just learned can certainly enhance the lecturing technique.

SUMMARY

As with any teaching method, lecturing can be effective or ineffective. We've all had the experience of sitting in the dreaded lecture with a monotone professor who reads from the book or from prepared notes. However, we have all also probably had the experience of being totally captivated by a professor who was sharing expertise and passion for the subject matter in a lecture. It is a myth that all lecturing is a passive experience where a professor transmits knowledge to a student. Lectures can be dynamic, interactive, engaging, and powerful. During a lecture, content can come alive for students. As previously noted, lectures are especially helpful in introductory courses or when students are fairly new to a field of study.

Now that we know some of the evidence behind the use of the lecture, it's time to explore how we can maximize learning via the lecture method of teaching. This book reviews several strategies to enhance student learning during lectures. In each chapter, the evidence behind each lecturing strategy is presented along with several practical suggestions to include active learning with the lecture. You'll find that the strategies are easy to incorporate into lectures, making immediate application likely. By incorporating some or all of the strategies discussed in this book, you will be helping your students master the content in your discipline.

REFERENCES

Baeten, M., Dochy, F., & Struyven, K. (2013). The effects of different learning environments on student's motivation for learning and their achievement. *British Journal of Educational Psychology, 83*, 484–501.

Bajak, A. (2014). *Lectures aren't just boring, they're ineffective, too, study finds.* Retrieved from http://news.sciencemag.org/education/2014/05/lectures-arent-just-boring-theyre-ineffective-too-study-finds

Barr, R. B., & Tagg, J. (1995). From teaching to learning—a new paradigm for undergraduate education. *Change, 27*(6), 12–25.

Barsade, S. G. (2016). The ripple effect: Emotional contagion and its influence on group behavior. *Administrative Science Quarterly, 47*, 644–675.

Beger, A. (2011). *Deliberate metaphors? An exploration of the choice and functions of metaphors in US-American college lectures.* Retrieved from https://www.academia.edu/934195/Deliberate_metaphors_An_exploration_of_the_choice_and_functions_of_metaphors_in_US-American_college_lectures

Berrett, D. (2012). How "flipping" the classroom can improve the traditional lecture. *Education Digest, 78*(1), 36–41.

Bligh, D. (2000). *What's the use of lectures?* San Francisco: CA: Jossey-Bass.

Brockliss, L. (1996). Curricula. In H. de Ridder-Symoens (Ed.), *A history of the university in Europe* (Vol. 11, pp. 565–620). Cambridge, England: Cambridge University Press.

Cangelosi, P. R., & Whitt, K. J. (2006). Teaching through storytelling: An examplar. *International Journal of Nursing Education Scholarship, 3*(1), 1–7.

Clark, R. E., Kirschner, P. A., & Sweller, J. (2012). Putting students on the path to learning: The case for fully guided instruction. *American Educator, 36*(1). 6–11.

Eagan, R. L. (1982). *Reading and comprehension.* Retrieved from ERIC database. (ED220819)

Evans, H. K. (2014). An experimental investigation of videotaped lectures in online courses. *Techtrends: Linking Research and Practice to Improve Learning, 58*(3), 63–70.

Freeman, S., Eddy, S. L., McDonough, M., Smith, M. K., Okoroafor, N., Jordt, H., & Wenderoth, M. P. (2014). Active learning increases student performance in science, engineering, and mathematics. *Proceedings of the National Academy of Sciences, 111*, 8410–8415. doi:10.1073/pnas.1319030111

Gold, R., & Faust, M. (2010). Right hemisphere dysfunction and metaphor comprehension in young adults with Asperger syndrome. *Journal of Autism and Developmental Disorders, 40*, 800–811. doi:10.1007/s10803-009-0930-1

Hake, R. (1998). Interactive-engagement vs. traditional methods: A six-thousand-student survey of mechanics test data for introductory physics courses. *American Journal of Physics, 66*, 64–74.

Hakeem, S. A. (2001). Effect of experiential learning in business statistics. *Journal of Education for Business, 77*(2), 95–98.

Hamilton, R. J. (1997). Effects of three types of elaboration on learning concepts from text. *Contemporary Educational Psychology, 22*, 299–318.

Handelsman, M. M. (2011, September 9). Is lecturing always unethical? *Psychology Today*. Retrieved from https://www.psychologytoday.com/blog/the-thical-professor/201109/is-lecturing-always-unethical

Harrington, C. (2016). *Student success in college. Doing what works!* (2nd ed.). Boston: MA: Cengage Learning.

Hrepic, Z., Zollman, D., & Rebello, N. (2007). Comparing students' and experts' understanding of the content of a lecture. *Journal of Science Education and Technology, 16*, 231–224.

Jensen, S. A. (2011). In-class versus online video lectures: Similar learning outcomes, but a preference for in-class. *Teaching of Psychology, 38*, 298–302.

Joordens, S., Le, A., Grinnell, R., & Chrysostomou, S. (2009). Eating your lectures and having them too: Is online lecture availability especially helpful in "skills-based" courses? *Electronic Journal of E-Learning, 7*, 281–288.

King, A. (1993). From sage on the stage to guide on the side. *College Teaching, 41*(1), 30–35.

King, A. (1995). Designing the instructional process to enhance critical thinking across the curriculum—Inquiring minds really do want to know: Using questioning to teach critical thinking. *Teaching of Psychology, 22*(1), 13–17.

Kirschner, P. A., Sweller, J., & Clark, R. E. (2006). Why minimal guidance during instruction does not work: An analysis of the failure of constructivist, discovery, problem-based, experiential, and inquiry-based teaching. *Educational Psychologist, 41*(2), 75–86.

Klahr, D., & Nigam, M. (2004). The equivalence of learning paths in early science instruction: Effects of direct instruction and discovery learning. *Psychological Science, 15*, 661–667. doi:10.1111/j.0956-7976.2004.00737.x

Lee, H. S., & Anderson J. R. (2013). Student learning: What's instruction got to do with it? *Annual Review of Psychology, 64*, 445–469.

Littlemore, J. (2001). The use of metaphor in university lectures and the problems that it causes for overseas students. *Teaching in Higher Education, 6*, 333–349. doi:10.1080/13562510120061205

Lordly, D. (2007). Once upon a time . . . Storytelling to enhance teaching and learning. *Canadian Journal of Dietetic Practice and Research, 68*(1), 30–35.

Major, C. H., Harris, M. S., & Zakrajsek, T. (2016). *Teaching for learning: 101 intentionally designed educational activities to put your students on the path to success*. New York, NY: Routledge.

Mayer, R. E. (2009). *Multi-media learning* (2nd ed.). New York: NY: Cambridge University Press.

Nasmith, L., & Steiner, Y. (2001). The evaluation of a workshop to promote interactive lecturing. *Teaching and Learning in Medicine, 13*(1), 43–48.

Pashler, H., McDaniel, M., Rohrer, D., & Bjork, R. (2008). Learning styles: Concepts and evidence. *Psychological Science in the Public Interest, 9*(3), 105–119. doi:10.1111/j.1539.6053.2009.01038

Regmi, K. (2012). A review of teaching methods—lecturing and facilitation in higher education (HE): A summary of the published evidence. *Journal of Effective Teaching, 12*(3), 61–76.

Snowball, J. (2014). Using interactive content and online activities to accommodate diversity in a large first year class. *Higher Education, 67*, 823–838. doi:10.1007/s10734-013-9708-7

Springer, L., Stanne, M., & Donovan, S. S. (1999). Effects of small-group learning on undergraduates in science, mathematics, engineering, and technology: A meta-analysis. *Review of Educational Research, 69*(1), 21–51.

Stacy, J. (2009). The guide on the stage: In defense of good lecturing in the history classroom. *Social Education, 73*, 275–278.

Toto, J., & Booth, K. (2008). Effects and implication of mini-lectures on learning in first-semester general chemistry. *Chemistry Education Research and Practice, 9*, 259–266.

Tuovinen, J. E., & Sweller, J. (1999). A comparison of cognitive load associated with discovery learning and worked examples. *Journal of Educational Psychology, 91*, 334–341. doi:10.1037/0022-0663.91.2.334

Woolfolk, A. (2013). *Educational psychology* (12th ed.). Boston, MA: Pearson Education.

2

TYPES OF LECTURES

THE SINGLE WORD LECTURE commonly elicits an image of an aging professor standing behind a lectern and droning on about some esoteric topic with students sitting in rows of seating appearing completely bored and disengaged. We laugh, cringe, and recall our own long class periods when viewing the famous scene from the 1986 movie *Ferris Bueller's Day Off* (Chinich et al., 1986) in which the teacher lectures on in a monotone voice while rhetorically asking questions, followed by "Anyone . . . . Anyone?" This scene notes the total student disengagement we typically ascribe to lecture-based classrooms. Lectures, as with any teaching strategy, can be poorly executed. It is important to note, however, that just as any teaching strategy can be done poorly, any teaching strategy can also be done effectively. The lecturing method has the potential to be very effective if executed well and paired appropriately with some learning-centered activities that require students' participation. One very important consideration in the discussion of effective lecturing is acknowledging that there are many different types of lectures, including paper-reading, storytelling, discussion-based, visually enhanced, demonstration, online, and interactive. Not all lectures are created equal. Each approach has pros and cons and may be selected based on factors such as the faculty member's knowledge of the content, motivation of students, material to be presented, and type of material to be learned.

As noted in Chapter 1, lectures are routinely branded as an ineffective method of instruction. The biggest challenge is that many individuals seem to lump all types of lectures into one specific type of lecture: reading a formal lecture to the class or presenting information in a low monotone voice. This type of lecture is commonly referred to as a formal or paper-reading lecture. As we contend in the following pages, there are vast differences in the types of lectures a faculty member may use. It would be very helpful in the area of teaching and learning to move away from the discussion about all lectures as if they were of one type and instead have discussions about which types of lectures are effective or ineffective and under which circumstances.

FORMAL OR PAPER-READING LECTURES

In the lecture, the professor typically stands behind the lectern and reads a paper or summary of the material to be learned. In essence, a prewritten formal speech is delivered to the students. This approach was common years ago at professional conferences, hence the phrase, "I am going to the conference to read (or present) a paper." Information is presented orally, and visual aids are not typically included with this lecture approach. Thus, the formal lecture style relies solely on communicating information via the auditory channel.

Advantages

The primary advantage of writing out the lecture as a speech before reading it to the class is that the product is often a well-organized, informative lecture. Another advantage is that the conversation is controlled, making it easier for faculty to deliver the content. Prior to reading the paper, a significant amount of time and energy is devoted to determining the most relevant and meaningful content, resulting in a strong organizational structure with main ideas and supporting details expressed articulately. Because formal paper-reading lectures are planned in advance, many perspectives and issues may be considered. For example, professors can include a variety of examples that would be meaningful and relevant to a diverse student population. With this approach, the content is typically focused on the most important topics, and off-task, presentation tangents are not likely to occur. Professors often turn to this lecturing approach when teaching classes with a significant amount of content because it can be an efficient way to share extensive content. As an expert, the professor is the one who best knows the content, and class time is used to accurately share course content with students. Important material is not left out when delivering the lecture, and students are also able to better determine how the professor thinks about the topic. The process of hearing a carefully constructed statement of information models good thinking in a given field of study. We have all seen accomplished lecturers use this method effectively. For example, the president of the United States will often passionately and skillfully read a speech on the state of the Union. The person using this style can still use strategies such as changing voice volume or pausing to draw attention to main points. Paper-reading lectures can certainly be eloquently written and read without many of the common verbal utterances such as "um" or "ah." Maintaining eye contact with the audience is important when reading a lecture to increase the audience's attention and engagement. To use this technique effectively, much practice is needed. It is therefore likely paper-reading lectures will improve over time.

Disadvantages

The main disadvantage of this approach is that students perceive the information as simply text they could easily read themselves. The one-directional approach can result in low attention, disengagement, and little actual learning. With this type of lecture, the professor is typically the only one speaking, and students may easily lose focus. It is often difficult for students to listen for extended periods of time without having an opportunity to digest and reflect on the information being heard. In other words, student engagement is particularly low with this type of lecture. The lack of visual aids can also make it difficult for students to maintain attention or get back on track if their attention drifts. A one-sensory approach (i.e., auditory) can make it challenging for students to learn the content because, according to some researchers, we learn best when a multisensory approach is used (Goswami, 2008). Although some professors can be engaging while reading a formal lecture, it is quite challenging to be so with this particular type of lecture. Many professors will not make much eye contact while reading, and this further reduces the attention and engagement of the students. A monotone voice is unfortunately also common with this approach, making it very difficult for students to differentiate the important from the less important content and to become excited about the content. The lack of opportunity for student involvement is particularly problematic. For example, there are not many invitations, if any at all, for students to ask or answer questions, leaving little to no room to foster student curiosity. Scripted lectures are also not as likely to promote critical thinking skills as strategies that typically promote higher level thinking (i.e., questioning and discussions) Paper-reading lectures delivered from behind a lectern instead typically focus on lower level cognitive skills such as remembering and understanding. Likewise, this lecturing approach does not allow students to benefit from interacting with classmates from various backgrounds who would likely have different perspectives and experiences that could enhance the learning process. In consideration of the disadvantages of the traditional lecture, it is typically best to use this method for very motivated and informed audiences, and even then limit the duration of each presentation.

STORYTELLING LECTURES

Storytelling has a long tradition of effective learning (Egan, 1998). The storytelling approach allows professors to identify characters or situations that provide meaning to the content. This narrative becomes the organizational structure for the lecture, with a beginning, a middle, and an end to the story. In other words, the example or context becomes the primary point of focus, and the course content is secondary in terms of organization. In many cases, mini stories or examples are used throughout the larger framework of the main story line. To better understand how the storytelling lecture approach differs from the formal paper-reading lecture, let's take a look at an example from psychology, such as different types of learning. Let's assume the lecture content is learning (e.g., classical conditioning, operational conditioning, and observational learning). In the paper-reading lecture, the professor may define key terms and then present several examples to illustrate each concept. In the storytelling approach, the professor would instead identify characters and a story, perhaps students in a second grade classroom. The professor would share information about the main characters and the setting. After setting the stage for the story line, examples that illustrate the learning concepts would be provided. For example, perhaps the professor would talk about how the teacher flicked the lights to move students from one learning activity to another, used a sticker chart with stars to encourage appropriate behaviors, and provided an example of one student's exemplary work. This would be followed by a timely description of classical conditioning, operant conditioning, and observational learning. In essence, the example would come before the content.

As with most stories, emotions play an important role. Faculty share their passion for the discipline through this storytelling approach. In most cases, stories are orally shared without the use of images, but faculty may opt to add visual images to enhance the learning experience. Although some faculty may use the lectern and notes for this approach, it is not typical. It is more common for the professor to tell the story without relying on notes. Rather than standing behind the lectern, most faculty using this approach walk around the room while telling their story. This promotes increased connection between the professor and students and can lead to higher levels of interest and engagement.

Advantages

Storytelling has stood the test of time as being an effective way to teach in a way that helps students to learn. When stories are engaging and relatable, students enjoy listening to them. Thus, it is often easy to capture and maintain the attention of students when using the storytelling lecture approach. Likewise, motivation for learning can be higher than with other lecture methods. The meaningful context in which the professor places the course content increases engagement and learning. The framework of using situations that students can relate to as a building block for adding new content knowledge to existing knowledge is an effective one. This strategy links learning to known experiences and prior knowledge and then expands on this knowledge base. The resulting elaboration of information results in increased new knowledge (Hernandez-Serrano & Stefanou, 2009). It is much easier for students to take in and learn content when the information is presented in a way that easily allows for connections to previously learned information. This is consistent with natural methods of learning in that new information is experienced within a frame of information already known, making the new information more meaningful and relevant to lived experiences. Everyone knows the frustration of being told a story containing information that is not known or has not been experienced previously. This underscores the importance of telling stories consistent with the backgrounds and experiences of students. When stories are consistent with the lived experiences of the students in the course, they are much more likely to recall content as it will be identified as meaningful and relevant.

Disadvantages

Although storytelling lectures can be a powerful approach to learning, it can be quite time consuming to create this type of lecture. A significant amount of time, energy, and creativity goes into the development of an effective story aligned with course content. It may also take longer to share the content with students as the professor will need to spend a significant amount of time setting the stage for the story line. Thus, this approach may result in less content coverage and may not work at all for some content. In addition, if students from diverse backgrounds have difficulty relating to the stories, this can have a negative impact on the learning process. It is therefore important to carefully choose story themes that will be meaningful to a diverse student body. Students may also struggle to discern the essential information portrayed in the story. This difficulty with transfer of information can be very challenging for novice learners who enjoy the story but fail to understand the content conveyed. As with the more formal paper-reading lecture style, visual images are not always used with this approach. Research has shown that students learn better when information is presented via multiple senses (Goswami, 2008). Thus, relying exclusively on the auditory channel may not lead to the best learning outcomes.

DISCUSSION-BASED LECTURES

Questions serve as the organizational structure for discussion-based lectures. With this approach, faculty assign readings prior to class, and students are expected to come to class ready to actively participate in a large-group discussion. In some cases, faculty provide guiding questions for each lecture ahead of time, and in other cases, the questions are posed during class. The lecture is interwoven into the discussion, often clarifying or expanding on student contributions. Sometimes the class begins with a brief lecture, which is followed by a question that sparks a large-group discussion. In most cases, professors carefully craft challenging questions that allow an in-depth exploration of the content. However, students may also be involved in developing the questions (King, 1995). In discussion-based lectures, students may volunteer to answer the question, or the professor may randomly call on students to answer questions. After the student responds to the question, the professor then provides validation and adds additional details via a lecture, uses the lecture to address inaccuracies and provides detailed explanations of concepts related to the question, or asks further questions to encourage a deeper look at the issues. Socratic questions, which are often used during discussion-based lectures, can be quite effective for promoting high-level thinking. Specifically, Socratic questions are designed to challenge assumptions, further explore evidence, or consider alternate perspectives (Paul, 1990; Strang, 2011).

Advantages

There is high level of student involvement in this lecture approach. Engagement with the content begins prior to class as preparation is needed to fully participate in the discussions. Because of the extra time devoted to learning and the active involvement of students during the discussion-based lecture, it is likely students will develop strong content knowledge as well as critical thinking skills. Students will have the benefit of hearing from classmates who may share different perspectives based on their varying cultural experiences. These different perspectives each serve as a memory cue, which makes it easier to retrieve the information at a later time. For example, if while discussing storage of individual memories, one colleague explains that memories are like stored books in a library, and another colleague in a discussion group explains that memories are like having multiple toolboxes in the garage that store individual tools, there are now retrieval cues based on books and toolboxes, both of which are familiar to most students. Because professors modify discussion-based lectures based on student interest or follow-up questions rather than following a rehearsed script, students often find this type of lecture more engaging, meaningful, and relevant than the more traditional lecture. Another advantage is that discussion-based lectures are flexible, giving students an opportunity to explore concepts of interest in more depth.

Disadvantages

Although questions posed during the lecture serve as an organizational structure, this type of lecture is much less structured than the traditional paper-reading lecture or the storytelling lecture. With questions targeting the key concepts from the course, it is easy to get off track and spend a significant amount of time on topics that may be of interest but may be less important or not aligned to the learning outcomes for the course. This lack of structure may result in missed content, particularly for more novice learners who may find it difficult to differentiate the important from the less important. This can be problematic in courses that serve as prerequisites to more advanced courses. With students who are novices in a given content area, it is also likely that some class time will be spent discussing inaccurate content. The discussion lecture method is dependent on students coming to class prepared with an accurate understanding of the assigned readings and ready to actively participate. When this is not the case, discussions are often not useful, and valuable class time can be wasted. It also assumes that students are comfortable participating in large class discussions, which may not be the case for all students. Although participation in class discussions is an important skill for students, it is important for the lecturer to be aware that many students struggle to participate in such discussions. Students who find participation difficult may well be identified as introverts, but others may struggle as well, such as shy students, those who have had bad experiences with class discussions, students with English as a second language, those from different cultures, and those who are less willing to take risks in front of others. As participating in discussion groups and speaking out in class is exhausting for some students, it is important to be mindful of this when this form of lecture is used.

VISUALLY ENHANCED LECTURES

Professors who lecture using visual aids integrate the use of slides or other visual tools into any form of lecture, which is a method commonly used. With this approach, the slides serve as a backdrop for the lecture content. Although there are many different visual tools available such as Prezi or Haiku Deck, PowerPoint continues to be the most commonly used tool for this purpose (Basturk, 2008). However, the specific tool used is less important than how it is used. Including a visual aid can increase learning by providing a relatable reference to the new information. We've come a long way from transparencies and overhead projectors and now have a vast array of visual tools available for this educational purpose. Images, Microsoft SmartArt, charts, graphs, and videos are just a few. With this approach, the professor lectures with the visual aid in the background, and throughout the lecture will often draw attention to the images being projected.

Advantages

Visual images are powerful aids to learning (Mayer, 2009). Visually enhanced lectures, if done well, can increase learning by helping students encode information via the auditory and visual channels rather than relying solely on the auditory channel. In addition to making it more likely that content will be learned using this multisensory approach, it will also be easier for students to later retrieve information learned. Visually enhanced aids are often well organized. As images can also distract from learning by drawing attention away from relevant content, faculty must think carefully about which images will best enhance the learning experience, which often results in a well-thought-out lecture in terms of organizational structure. Research has shown that sharing the slides with students ahead of class is associated with increased learning (Marsh & Sink, 2010). The visual aid is therefore not just a resource during class but can also help the student outside class. The visual aid can also make it easier for students to get back on track when their attention drifts.

Disadvantages

Although the high level of organization often associated with this lecture method can be an advantage, it can also be a disadvantage. Sometimes faculty adhere to the slide presentation in a rigid fashion, not allowing student questions and interest to shape the lecture. The other problem with this approach relates to pacing. In the chalk-and-talk days when professors wrote on the board instead of using PowerPoint slides, the lesson progressed at a slower pace because the professor had to spend time writing or drawing on the board, thus creating natural pauses during the lecture. With PowerPoint or other similar tools, the professor may go too quickly, not giving students time to digest and reflect on the content. By providing students with printed copies of the slides, this problem can be minimized because students won't feel a need to copy the content of each slide (Marsh & Sink, 2010), but professors will still need to be mindful of the pacing of the lecture when using slides.

Perhaps the biggest disadvantages occur not because of this method itself but rather because it has not been used effectively in a great number of instances (Kosslyn, Kievit, Russell, & Shephard, 2012). If poorly executed (e.g., slides of endless text and bullet points), the lecture with visual aids method can have a negative impact on learning (Isseks, 2011). For example, Mayer (2009) described the redundancy principle, in which students are faced with information from two sources (e.g., listening to the professor and reading the slide), and how this negatively affects the learning process because it's not possible to listen and read at the same time. Thus, having a slide that consists of primarily words may do more harm than good.

DEMONSTRATION LECTURES

Demonstration lectures consist of a professor illustrating how to complete a task while explaining it. This type of lecture is frequently used in science, technology, engineering, and math, but of course it can work well in many other disciplines where it would be helpful for students to see a problem or situation as it is being discussed. For instance, a math professor can show students the steps involved in a complicated math problem, or a professor in the sciences may describe how to engage in safe laboratory practices while demonstrating how to properly use safety gear. In a chemistry course, an instructor can show how to mix two dangerous chemicals. Professors using this approach will often conduct live demonstrations as needed during the lecture, but some will also include brief video demonstrations. With new technologies, such as simulations, more and more faculty may rely on integrating technology-based demonstrations into lectures. When videos are used, the professor will often pause the video to provide further explanation, make connections to content previously learned, or highlight important information. Thus, the video doesn't replace the lecture but rather augments it. After conducting the demonstration, students are often provided with an opportunity to apply what was learned to a similar problem or situation. This practice opportunity can be incorporated into the lecture, in a separate lab session, or assigned as homework.

Advantages

We can learn a tremendous amount from watching others (Bandura 1977). Balch's (2014) research showed that students who viewed a demonstration outperformed students who only listened to a lecture. Adding a powerful demonstration component to the lecture provides students with a richer, more meaningful learning experience. The lecture content will immediately be relevant to a student's subsequent problem or situation. In demonstration lectures, the learning and engagement levels are high. It is typical for professors to ask students to explore solving a similar problem or situation after the demonstration. This provides students with an opportunity to transfer the knowledge and skills just learned to a different situation, which is a strategy that undoubtedly enhances the learning experience. Demonstrations may be live or virtual. Research has found that although students prefer live demonstrations, virtual demonstrations can be just as effective (Lewis, 2015).

Disadvantages

Although the demonstration lecture is an extremely effective method, demonstrations take a significant amount of planning and class time. Faculty will need to spend much time and energy determining which problems or situations are best suited for the demonstration, decide whether a live or technology-based demonstration will work best, and then prepare to conduct the demonstration. Because demonstrations can take a lot of time to conduct during class, there is less time for content coverage, resulting in students needing to learn additional course content on their own outside class.

ONLINE LECTURES

Given the increase in online courses, it is important to also consider online lectures. As with face-to-face lectures, there are many different formats and types of online lectures. Most online lectures are much shorter in duration than lectures that take place in traditional classrooms, but they can be the same length or even longer. A common lecture format is a narrated PowerPoint presentation, which is basically a slide show with the professor verbally explaining the content. In some cases, faculty may opt to use a webcam when developing online lectures. Some video editing programs such as Screencast-O-Matic or TechSmith Camtasia allow you to show a small video of yourself in the corner of the screen at the same time the PowerPoint slides are presented. However, research has found that the professor's visual image may not be needed. Specifically, Dey, Burn, and Gerdes (2009) found no significant difference in student learning when students viewed a narrated PowerPoint presentation with and without the instructor's image. However, students without the image did report that they would have preferred seeing the professor's image, and those who did see the image said it was not distracting. Several programs such as Office Mix, a PowerPoint add-in, or Adobe Captivate allow you to add interactive elements such as quizzes.

It should be noted that the research on the effectiveness of online lectures is mixed. Jensen (2011) found that online lectures were as effective as in-person lectures. Williams, Birch, and Hancock (2012) found that online lectures as a supplement were valuable. When lectures were posted online as a resource, 80% of the students thought these were valuable resources, and 60% of students said they viewed the lectures prior to attending the next class (Odhabi & Nicks-McCaleb, 2011). However, other studies have not found benefits connected to the availability of online lectures to students (Evans, 2014; Joordens, Le, Grinnell, & Chrysostomou, 2009).

Many video options can be used as online lectures. Sometimes faculty use open source videos from the Web as the lecture. In other cases, faculty create their own personalized online lectures for the course. McGovern and Baruca (2013) conducted an important study in which they found that personalized videos created by the professor worked best. Students not only prefered for their professor to create the video but also performed better on a quiz related to the video content when they viewed a video created by their professor. Although there are many advocates of using open source materials in college courses, this research illustrates the importance of the presence of the professor and how the professor-student relationship can play an important role in learning.

Screencasts are another option where the faculty member may deliver an online demonstration on how to use a technology tool. Screencasts display the actions on a computer screen while the professor narrates, explains, or demonstrates the steps needed to complete a task. Many faculty members create narrated screencasts as an orientation to the course, showing students where to find course materials and how the learning management system works, but they can be used for a variety of other purposes. For example, an instructor can show students how to search library databases or how to use a computer program. Screencasts can also be used to record PowerPoint presentations, and a webcam can be used to include a video component. Research has found that screencasts increase learning (Lloyd, & Robertson, 2012). As previously discussed in the section on demonstration lectures, we learn a lot when watching someone else perform a task.

Videos are another option for online lectures. Most professors using this option create videos specifically for online courses, but sometimes they may opt to have their traditional classes videotaped and posted online as a supplemental resource. Videos created for online courses are often brief, typically ranging from 5 to 15 minutes for each topic. Thomson, Bridgstock, and Willems (2014) argue that short videos are best because students will likely stop watching videos they perceive to be too long. Watching online lectures is usually not as engaging as watching a live lecture, and students are typically watching the video in an environment where multitasking temptations are prevalent. Videos may be created using simple tools such as the video feature on phones or more professionally using media services with a videographer. Informal videos are often not edited, but professional, more formal videos may be edited and enhanced with additional features. Professors may also choose to use videos that already exist, such as TED talks, to replace or augment instructor-created videos.

Advantages

One of the primary advantages of posting a lecture online is that students can watch the lecture as many times as needed. This is particularly helpful to students who have learning challenges or for students whose native language is not English. Online lectures are a good platform for faculty to share their expertise with students. In addition to serving as a primary resource in online courses, they can be a supportive resource for students in traditional courses. When quizzes or other interactive tools are embedded into lectures using programs such as Office Mix, faculty can assess how well students are understanding the lecture content. Another advantage of online lectures is that once you have recorded the lecture, you can use this lecture again in future classes, assuming the content is still relevant and up to date. The use of online demonstrations with videos or screencasts is a great way for students to learn through observation without using valuable class time. Thus, class time can be used for other engaging learning activities.

Disadvantages

Narrated PowerPoint presentations do provide students with an incredibly helpful resource above and beyond the textbook, but they are not as engaging as in-person lectures. Videos can be more engaging than narrated PowerPoint presentations, but they often lack visual aids. Videos of only the professor talking do not fully take advantage of the visual power of a video (Thomson et al., 2014). It is also important to note that online resources need to be accessible, and it can be extremely time consuming and costly to caption all the online videos, although prices are decreasing rapidly. Writing a script ahead of time can make the captioning process easier, but this often results in a less engaging presentation. Online lectures that do not have scripts are often more natural, but they also often have more fillers such as "um," and transcribing these videos can be an onerous task. However, it is important for course materials, including online lectures, to be in compliance with accessibility regulations.

Although online lectures can be an efficient method for covering course content, built-in opportunities to apply and engage with the content are often not available, limited in nature, or are quite time consuming to develop. In addition, the instructor cannot see the nonverbal and verbal reactions of students, which may be the biggest disadvantage. Without immediate feedback, it is difficult to know if the pacing of the material is appropriate and what information is being understood and what information may be confusing. When lecturing in a traditional in-person environment, faculty often make real-time modifications as needed based on feedback from students. In other words, if students look confused, additional explanations and examples can be offered.

Developing online lectures is a very time-consuming process, and it can be much more difficult to integrate new research or current examples into online lectures as compared to live lectures. For example, faculty members teaching in-person courses will often make connections between course content and recent stories in the news. Updating online lectures involves either redoing the entire video or learning how to edit the video. Once the edits are made, captioning will also need to be updated. Because this is an overwhelming task, many professors may put off updating the online lectures, making them dated and less relevant.

INTERACTIVE LECTURES

Interactive lectures are a combination of lecturing and brief, active learning opportunities. Any of the previously noted types of lectures may have an interactive component. Professors using interactive strategies typically lecture for a portion of the class time and then provide students with an opportunity to apply the content. This process is often repeated several times throughout the class period. A variety of brief, active learning strategies can be used after each lecture segment. We'll be discussing many of these strategies in detail throughout the book. A few examples include having students talk to one another to summarize the content or identify a relevant application or example, write a summary of what was learned, or share and compare notes with a classmate. The interactive opportunities are typically very brief, using just a minute or so of class time, but they could be longer, with more involved applications taking 20 to 30 minutes or even more. After this interactive activity, the professor returns to lecturing to address another topic, and then a different active learning opportunity is used to help students digest and apply the newly learned content.

Interactive strategies are not solely used after each lecture segment. They can also be used within the lecture itself. For instance, professors may ask and answer questions, conducting comprehension checks, which is a powerful way to gather data that can guide the rest of the lecture (Hogan, Rabinowitz, & Craven, 2003). If students are understanding concepts, the professor can move on to new content. If, however, students are struggling with the material, the professor can provide additional examples or present the information in a different way. Clickers or applications can be used to quickly gauge learning levels. The Poll Everywhere app and the game-based Kahoot! platform are two examples of polling technologies that can be integrated into a PowerPoint presentation. The results will be immediately shared on the screen, providing real-time data on whether the students are grasping the content. In addition, research has found empirical support for the use of clickers in the classroom (Hoekstra & Mollborn, 2012).

Advantages

Interactive lecturing has long been shown to be very effective (Hake, 1998; Crouch & Mazur, 2001). The student has the opportunity to immediately practice, or implement, background knowledge just learned by listening to the expert lecture. Because the lecture is focused and brief, typically about 15 to 20 minutes, it is relatively easy to maintain students' attention. When polling or other similar active strategies are used during the lecture portion, attention and engagement are even more likely. An additional benefit of this approach is that it translates into a more flexible lecture where the professor is using real-time feedback and data to make immediate modifications to the lecture. Using feedback to make adjustments is a learning-centered approach. The use of interactive techniques after the brief lectures further promotes engagement and learning. Being able to immediately digest and apply the content via a brief activity results in higher levels of learning (Drabick, Weisberg, Paul, & Bubier, 2007). As many of these interactive opportunities involve working with a partner or small group, the benefits extend beyond content knowledge. Transferable skills such as problem-solving can be learned using the interactive lecture (Gülpinar & Yeğen, 2005). This approach can also assist students with developing essential communication and collaboration skills and promote stronger connections among students. In addition, these interactive pauses during the lecture give students an opportunity to engage with classmates from varying backgrounds. This is beneficial because it not only increases appreciation for different personal and cultural beliefs but also can promote the development of critical thinking skills (Pascarella, Palmer, Moye, & Pierson, 2001; Schreiber & Valle, 2013). Thus, a true sense of a community can be established via the numerous opportunities for interaction.

Disadvantages

The primary concern of faculty is that implementing interactions in the classroom takes time, which reduces the amount of information that can be covered. That said, research consistently shows that these insertions increase overall learning (e.g., Hake, 1998). Unfortunately, planning an interactive lecture can take a significant amount of time, energy, and expertise. Rather than a one-, two-, or three-hour lecture, faculty will need to think about how to break down their long lecture into meaningful, shorter lecture segments. In addition, faculty will need to know what interactive techniques will best assist students with learning the content and may need training on how to use these techniques. Another possible disadvantage is that students may shift to off-task conversations and behaviors during the interactive opportunities. It will therefore be important to monitor students during the active learning exercises, a task that is more challenging in large lecture halls. If students are participating in off-task behaviors, this will not result in positive outcomes.

SUMMARY

When speaking of the effectiveness of the lecture method, many individuals have a prototypic image in mind of a faculty member standing behind a lectern droning on in a monotone voice with little enthusiasm for the subject. As noted in this chapter, there are many very different forms a lecture may take, and within each of the forms there are effective and less effective ways to deliver the information. When considering how best to convey new information to students, it is helpful to consider the advantages and disadvantages of the different types of lectures, focusing on how to best increase student engagement and learning.

REFERENCES

Balch, W. R. (2014). A referential communication demonstration versus a lecture-only control: Learning benefits. *Teaching of Psychology, 41*, 213–219. doi:10.1177/0098628314537970

Bandura, A. (1977). *Social learning theory*. Englewood Cliffs, NJ: Prentice Hall.

Basturk, R. (2008). Applying the many-facet Rasch model to evaluate PowerPoint presentation performance in higher education. *Assessment & Evaluation in Higher Education, 33*(4), 1–14. doi:10.1080/02602930701562775

Chinich, M., Hughes, J., Jacobson, T., Vickerilla, J. (Producers), & Hughes, J. (Director). (1986). *Ferris Bueller's day off* [Motion picture]. United States: Paramount Pictures.

Crouch, C. H., & Mazur, E. (2001). Peer instruction: Ten years of experience and results. *American Journal of Physics*, 69, 970–977.

Dey, E. L., Burn, H. E., & Gerdes, D. (2009). Bringing the classroom to the Web: Effects of using new technologies to capture and deliver lectures. *Research in Higher Education*, 50, 377–393.

Drabick, D. A. G., Weisberg, R., Paul, L, & Bubier, J. L. (2007). Methods and techniques: Keeping it short and sweet: Brief, ungraded writing assignments facilitate learning. *Teaching of Psychology, 34*, 172–176.

Egan, K. (1985). Teaching as story-telling: A non-mechanistic approach to planning teaching. *Journal of Curriculum Studies, 17*, 397–406.

Evans, H. K. (2014). An experimental investigation of videotaped lectures in online courses. *TechTrends*, 58(3), 63–70.

Goswami, U. (2008). Principles of learning, implications for teaching: A cognitive neuroscience perspective. *Journal of Philosophy of Education*, 42, 381–399.

Gülpinar, M. A., & Yeğen, B. Ç. (2005). Interactive lecturing for meaningful learning in large groups. *Medical Teacher, 27*, 590–594. doi:10.1080/01421590500136139

Hake, R. (1998). Interactive-engagement vs. traditional methods: A six-thousand-student survey of mechanics test data for introductory physics courses. *American Journal of Physics, 66*, 64–74.

Hernandez-Serrano, J., Stefanou, S. E. (2009). Knowledge at work: Learning and transferring expert reasoning skills through storytelling. *Education, Knowledge & Economy*, 3(1), 55–81.

Hoekstra, A., & Mollborn, S. (2012). How clicker use facilitates existing pedagogical practices in higher education: Data from interdisciplinary research on student response systems. *Learning, Media And Technology, 37*, 303–320. doi:10.1080/17439884.2011.568493

Hogan, T., Rabinowitz, M., & Craven, J. A. (2003). Representation in teaching: Inferences from research on expert and novice teachers. *Educational Psychologist, 38*, 235–247.

Isseks, M. (2011). How PowerPoint is killing education. *Educational Leadership, 68*(5), 74–76.

Jensen, S. A. (2011). In-class versus online video lectures: Similar learning outcomes, but a preference for in-class. *Teaching of Psychology, 38*, 298–302.

Joordens, S., Le, A., Grinnell, R., & Chrysostomou, S. (2009). Eating your lectures and having them too: Is online lecture availability especially helpful in "skills-based" courses?. *Electronic Journal of E-Learning, 7*, 281–288.

King, A. (1995). Designing the instructional process to enhance critical thinking across the curriculum—Inquiring minds really do want to know: Using questioning to teach critical thinking. *Teaching of Psychology, 22*, 13–17.

Kosslyn, S. M., Kievit, R. A., Russell, A. G., & Shephard, J. M. (2012). PowerPoint® presentation flaws and failures: A psychological analysis. *Frontiers in Psychology, 3*. doi:10.3389/fpsyg.2012.00230

Lewis, J. L. (2015). A comparison between two different activities for teaching learning principles: Virtual animal labs versus human demonstrations. *Scholarship of Teaching and Learning in Psychology, 1*, 182–188. doi:10.1037/stl0000013

Lloyd, S. A., & Robertson, C. L. (2012). Screencast tutorials enhance student learning of statistics. *Teaching of Psychology, 39*, 67–71. doi:10.1177/0098628311430640

Marsh, E. J., & Sink, H. E. (2010). Access to handouts of presentation slides during lecture: Consequences for learning. *Applied Cognitive Psychology, 24*, 691–706. doi:10.1002/acp.1579

Mayer, R. E. (2009). *Multi-media learning* (2nd ed.). New York, NY: Cambridge University Press.

McGovern, E., & Baruca, A. (2013). Want to enroll in a MOOC? No thanks, my professors have their own videos. *Journal for Advancement of Marketing Education, 21*(2), 64–76.

Odhabi, H., & Nicks-McCaleb, L. (2011). Video recording lectures: Student and professor perspectives. *British Journal of Educational Technology, 42*, 327–336. doi:10.1111/j.1467-8535.2009.01011.x

Pascarella, E., Palmer, B., Moye, M., & Pierson, C. (2001). Do diversity experiences influence the development of critical thinking? *Journal of College Student Development, 42*, 257–271.

Paul, R. (1990). *Critical thinking: What every person needs to survive in a rapidly changing world.* Rohnert Park, CA: Center for Critical Thinking and Moral Critique.

Schreiber, L. M., & Valle, B. (2013). Social constructivist teaching strategies in the small group classroom. *Small Group Research, 44*, 395-411. doi:10.1177/1046496413488422.

Strang, K. (2011). How can discussion forum questions be effective in online MBA courses? *Campus-Wide Information Systems, 28*(2), 80–92.

Thomson, A., Bridgstock, R., & Willems, C. (2014). "Teachers flipping out" beyond the online lecture: Maximising the educational potential of video. *Journal of Learning Design*, *7*(3), 67–78.

Williams, A., Birch, E., & Hancock, P. (2012). The impact of online lecture recordings on student performance. *Australasian Journal of Educational Technology*, *28*, 199–213.

PART TWO

ENHANCING LECTURES

3

ACTIVATING PRIOR KNOWLEDGE

BARR AND TAGG (1995) noted the importance of shifting the focus of education from teaching to learning. Understanding the learning process helps us identify teaching strategies that will assist students with learning and applying new information. Knowledge is cumulative, and learning new information is heavily influenced by what is already known. For more than 100 years psychologists have held that prior information is extremely important in the learning process (e.g., Baldwin, 1898; James, 1890). With recent advances in cognitive neuroscience, prior knowledge has been shown to be even more important than previously thought (Willingham, 2009). For many decades, the strongest psychological models proposed a relatively simple three-step process (Atkinson & Shiffrin, 1968). According to this information processing model, new information arrived through your senses (sensory memory), and if attended to, the information made its way to short-term memory. If the information was not attended to, it was lost. The attended to information was thought to be held in short-term memory for roughly 20 seconds, long enough to process the information in some way. Here, content would either be immediately put to use in some way or lost. If the student actively worked with the content, then it was believed the content would have a good chance of making it into long-term memory where it could stay forever. A generation of learners were taught this relatively simple one-directional model of memory. This model has evolved over time because of our increased understanding of the interactive nature of how memory works (Willingham, 2009). Thus, although many of the core elements of Atkinson and Shiffrin (1968) model still serve as a useful framework, it is important that our understanding of memory reflects current research.

Research has shown that learning is incremental (Goswami, 2008) and that our experiences and knowledge influence what we perceive to be important or not important (Willingham, 2009). The original Atkinson and Shiffrin (1968) memory model focused on how information moved from one stage to the next, not why it was attended to in the first place. As we encounter new stimuli, our brain quickly scans and searches our long-term memory to help decide whether this new information is worthwhile and needed. Thus, new content coming in through our senses is not all treated the same; some information will get preferential treatment because of our past experiences (Snyder, Holder, Weintraub, Carter, & Alain, 2009). Researchers have found that we are indeed influenced by our prior experiences and knowledge as we learn new content (Heit, 1994).

Another significant change in our understanding of memory relates to what Atkinson and Shiffrin (1968) called *short-term memory*, which began to be referred to as *working memory* (Baddeley & Hitch, 1974). Working memory has been determined to be a more accurate descriptor of what happens during this stage because we are working with new content in hopes of retaining it. Baddeley and Hitch (1974) argued that working memory is complex, with subsystems working together in an interactive manner to help us learn new content. However, much of the short-term language is still accurate and meaningful. For example, we are limited in how much content we can work with at a time. In classic studies by Miller (1956), it was demonstrated that we are only able to hold on to and work with about seven chunks of information at a time. In addition, we quickly lose the new content coming in if we do not actively use it in some way. Thus, our working memory is limited, meaning we can only work with a few new concepts at once. It is also important to note that we do not have long to hold on to information in working memory, often less than 30 seconds, unless we are actively using the information. Using effective memory strategies such as imagery and elaboration in this part of the process is therefore necessary (Unsworth, 2016). This also demonstrates why it is important to periodically have students in class apply the information just learned.

The primary challenge in learning is moving information from working memory to long-term memory. One of the most important factors in getting information into long-term memory, and there are many, is our prior or related knowledge. It is much easier to learn new information that is related to content we already know than to learn something totally new. During the working memory part of the memory process, we search our long-term memory for any previously stored knowledge or experiences that are relevant or meaningful (Baddeley, 2002).

If we discover that we do know information about the topic, we make connections with our previous knowledge, building neural networks through a process called *elaboration* (Schwartz, Son, Kornell, & Finn, 2011). These connections to previously established neural pathways increase learning, as they allow us to build on what we already know. If, however, we search our long-term memory and do not find any related content or experiences, neural pathways must be built from scratch, a more time-consuming and cumbersome process (Cameron, 1993). This explains why experts are able to take in and learn new information faster and with less effort than novices; they have many more prior experiences and significantly more knowledge that allows additional connections to be made to new information and skills being learned. Their long-term memory is a gold mine of information, making it very easy to attach new content to previously learned content. Novices, in contrast, do not have already established neural pathways, so they need to work hard at creating new neural pathways and building connections as they learn new content. Sometimes novice learners may have relevant information in their long-term memory, but the connection between the new content and the previously learned content may not always be obvious (Goswami, 2008). Experts not only have more information to work with, but also are able to more easily identify the possible connections between new and old information. This is why it is so helpful when faculty, who are the experts, explicitly point out connections that may not be immediately apparent to students. Thus, prior knowledge on a subject matter directly affects how we take in and learn new information. Sterner and Wedman (1996) demonstrated that prior experience with solving problems also influenced the learning process. Thus, what we have learned previously helps us learn new information.

If information is successfully moved to our long-term memory, there is no limit to the length of time the information or skill may be retained. Individuals who are 80 or more years of age may well recall events or information from their childhood with amazing accuracy. Long-term memory is limitless with respect to capacity, meaning we can store as much information as we want or need. It is impossible to fill our long-term memory. However, it may be difficult to find or retrieve information when needed, especially if we have not stored it in a way that promotes easy access. Storing the content in an organized fashion will help us retrieve the information when we need it. Think about how much easier it is to find your document files on your computer if you have clearly titled folders and subfolders. If all of your files are in one giant miscellaneous folder or on your computer desktop, it is much more difficult, sometimes even impossible, to find a specific file. The categories used to mentally organize information we encode are often referred to as *schemas*. Piaget, a developmental psychologist, coined the term *schema* and talked about how schemas change based on our learning experiences (Woolfolk, 2013). When we learn, we modify existing schemas to accommodate the new information or create additional schemas to house the new content. Our schemas therefore increase and grow in complexity as we learn.

The more frequently we access or use specific content, the easier it will be to retrieve it when needed at a later time. By retrieving information over and over again, we're building strong, efficient neural pathways that make the information easily accessible. In addition, prior knowledge increases the likelihood of our using more efficient parts of the brain for learning. In a fascinating study, van Kesteren and colleagues (2014) examined brain activities during learning. In this study, second-year undergraduate students underwent fMRIs (functional magnetic resonance imaging) while they were learning new content. Some of the content was based on previously learned content (prior knowledge), whereas other content was unrelated to material previously covered. Participants in the study with prior knowledge about the new content being learned were more likely to process this information using efficient brain functions, which led to increased learning (van Kesteren, Rijpkema, Ruiter, Morris, & Fernàndez, 2014).

Having adequate background knowledge not only is important during lectures but also can significantly affect other academic tasks. Reading, one of the primary avenues for learning, is an important example. The role of prior knowledge in reading comprehension was investigated in a classic study by Recht and Leslie (1988). In this study, students were placed into groups based on whether they were poor or good readers and whether they had high or low content knowledge about baseball. The students were asked to read a passage on baseball, answer questions about the passage, and re-create the story nonverbally. Not surprisingly, overall, the good readers who had high baseball knowledge performed the best, and poor readers who had low baseball knowledge performed the worst on a comprehension test. The fascinating finding, however, was that the poor readers with high baseball knowledge performed almost as well as the good readers with high baseball knowledge, and the good readers with low baseball knowledge performed almost as poorly as the poor readers with low baseball knowledge. Knowledge of baseball was more important than reading proficiency when reading a passage and then answering questions about that information (Recht & Leslie, 1988). Thus, this finding highlights the importance of background knowledge in being able to take in and comprehend new information via reading. In fact, this research demonstrates that prior knowledge matters more than reading skills. The importance of prior knowledge has also been found in other academic tasks such as improved note-taking skills (Wetzels, Kester, van Merrienboer, & Broers, 2011).

Given this understanding of how memory works, activating students' prior knowledge on the subject being taught will help students take in the content in a way that is more efficient and effective. Often students will have some background knowledge on a topic, but for a variety of reasons, this information doesn't jump out at students as they are searching their long-term memory for help with learning new content. It may be that the needed content has not been retrieved often so the neural pathway isn't as accessible, or it could be that as novice learners, students do not immediately recognize how the prior knowledge may be connected or related to the new content. This is where your assistance as the professor is needed to help students to process information presented during lectures.

As the expert in the subject matter, you play a key role in helping students identify what type of information might prove helpful in learning the new information. For example, if students don't have much prior knowledge on how memory works but do have a basic understanding of computers, professors can help students access their knowledge on how information is stored using a computer as an example. This knowledge can then be used to help facilitate new learning. For instance, students will likely be able to understand how the computer temporarily stores what is written in a document, but it is not stored permanently until it is officially saved. This analogy can be used to help students understand the difference between working and long-term memory. Although analogies such as this one can be incredibly helpful to some students, they can also negatively affect the learning experience for students who are not familiar with the related concept. We must always be mindful that examples used in our lectures may not resonate with students who are significantly younger than we are, come from different cultures, or for whom English is not their first language (Littlemore, 2001). Knowing what your students know will help you identify relevant information that will assist students with taking in new information. As the professor, you also have the opportunity to build knowledge as the course progresses. Thus, students at the end of a course will be able to use information learned at the beginning of the course to help them take in the new content. This will also be the case with courses that have prerequisites. In other words, you are building background knowledge every day with your students, and this knowledge will serve them well as they continue learning throughout their college experience and in life.

LECTURE ENHANCEMENT STRATEGIES

Activating prior knowledge is a key consideration in helping students learn new information, and there are several ways to promote this activation during a lecture. The following strategies are designed to assist you in helping students activate their prior knowledge. If you already use some of these lecture enhancement strategies, think of ways to adapt them for future use.

Pretest

A pretest is an effective method to assess what students already know about the subject for two primary reasons. First, it provides you with a good overview of what the students in the class know and don't know about the subject, including whether students have previously learned inaccurate information. If students have an inaccurate knowledge base, this can make new learning very difficult. Although it is certainly possible to unlearn the content, this is more difficult than simply learning new content. Challenging faulty thinking takes much time and effort. The information you discover about accurate and inaccurate prior knowledge, or the absence of prior knowledge, can be used to develop effective lectures and lecture activities. The second primary reason for this technique is that engaging students in the retrieval practice of previously learned content brings immediate attention to this content. In essence, you have activated relevant prior knowledge so that it is more readily accessible to the student and will aid the student in learning new content in the future. This type of activity might be particularly important if you are teaching a course with a prerequisite. If the content learned in previous courses is essential to the new content you'll be presenting, it will be important for you to know how well your students understand the prerequisite material. A pretest can guide how you proceed. It may be necessary to provide students with online support materials to help them refresh their memory for this content, or you may even need to devote some class time to review previously covered material.

Quick Quizzes

Quizzing at the start of a semester provides you with helpful information about the current knowledge base of students in your class. Quizzing throughout the semester prior to starting a given type of lecture for the day is an effective way to continually activate prior knowledge and monitor students' learning progress. It also provides an excellent opportunity for students to retrieve previously stored information so that it is very accessible as they strive to learn the new material. It puts the previous content front and center, so when you introduce new concepts in the lecture students won't have to look too far to make connections to material recently covered. Quizzes could occur before class using online tools, at the beginning of class, or at any point within the class period. Although formal quizzes are valuable, informal quizzing can also be quite helpful. Informal quizzes are typically brief and are often not graded. Polling software, such as Poll Everywhere and Kahoot!, or classroom clickers allow students to take brief quizzes using technology tools, and the responses from the class can then be displayed on the board and integrated into your lecture. These tools make it very easy for you to assess how well students are learning your course content and activate this prior knowledge so they are ready to take in the new course content you are about to present. If you or your students don't have access to technology or are in a space where technology is limited, you can use no-tech options for polling or quick quizzes. For example, you can ask students to raise their hand to respond to a true-or-false or multiple-choice quiz question or ask students to raise colored index cards representing the different answer choices. Regardless of the method you select, quick quizzes activate prior knowledge and provide you with incredibly useful information as you continue to lecture on a topic.

Dusting Off the Cobwebs

Sometimes you'll discover that students' background knowledge is so limited or even nonexistent it makes activating prior knowledge almost impossible. Although this may be the case on the very first day of class, it is a short-lived problem. Once you've had the opportunity to build some background knowledge through your lessons, you can help students activate content you have taught them. The dusting-off-the-cobwebs exercise is a great way to activate prior knowledge at the start of class prior to starting the lecture strategy for the day. For this exercise, you can assign partners or students can self-select their partners; however, changing partners every time you do the activity is recommended. In the starting step of the exercise, ask students to discuss what they learned during the previous class (or reading assignments) without using their notes or books. Give students about two minutes. Next, students open their notebooks and textbooks and discuss with their partner any content they forgot or missed. In essence, they are filling in the information gaps. Give them another two minutes for this step. The final step is a large-group review where you randomly call on students to briefly share a concept from the prior class or from the reading assignment. Randomly calling on students helps keep students on task during this activity. Most students, even those who may not be frequent participants, are comfortable sharing their ideas after this activity because they had four minutes to think about and discuss the content. It is therefore a relatively safe strategy to use with students who may not typically contribute to class discussions. If you are going to randomly call on students, inform them prior to beginning the exercise so students will expect to be called on. This large-group review typically takes about five minutes, depending on the complexity of the concepts, the level of student understanding, and the depth of the review. Because this activity takes about 10 minutes in its entirety, you might use it once per week rather than during every class period. In addition to activating their prior knowledge, this dusting-off-the-cobwebs activity also provides you with quick assessment data about how well students understand the concepts previously presented. If you discover information gaps or inaccuracies, you can review material in more depth before addressing the new content in the upcoming lesson. It is a powerful way to begin a class. You can also use this strategy at the beginning of a course that has prerequisite requirements. You can make a list of the most important concepts or theories they should have been previously exposed to in the prerequisite course, then ask students to discuss with a partner what they remember about these concepts. Finally, you can have a large-group review of the material.

This activity is called *dusting off the cobwebs* because it shows students that with a little cognitive cleaning, the information can be found in long-term memory. It is common for students to start off not remembering much, especially when using prior course material, but they can very quickly shift to remembering when others start to discuss the content. The discussion of the content triggers the retrieval process, and information previously learned has now been activated.

What Do I Know? Turn and Talk

The turn-and-talk activity is focused on helping students identify potentially useful experiences that may aid the learning process. For this activity, ask students to turn to a nearby classmate and talk about what the classmate already knows or thinks he or she knows about the content that will soon be the focus of the lecture. Encourage students to consider previously learned course content, as well as personal experiences that may relate to the content or serve as examples of concepts. The purpose is to give students an opportunity to activate prior knowledge that might assist with learning the new content. This activity can be brief; even allowing only two to three minutes for this task can have positive results. While they are engaged in this activity, walk around the classroom to hear the connections they are making and then assist students who are having difficulty identifying possible connections. After students have had the opportunity to discuss what prior experiences might connect to the new content, you can ask for volunteers to share the connections they found and then expand on these concepts. You can also use this information to guide you as you lecture on this new content. Referring to the content they already know during the lecture can help them make connections and increase their learning. In other words, take notes on the examples they discuss and refer to these examples at appropriate times during the lecture.

Explicit Links

One very simple yet effective strategy is to remind students of previous content that is related to the new content you are about to present. For example, when discussing a new theory, you can make references to a theory they learned the previous week. Explicitly explaining how the theories are similar or different can help students learn the content. Although many of us do this naturally during lectures, it is important to also formally incorporate this strategy into the planning process. In other words, when developing a lecture, think about explicit connections that will help your students master the content. Remember, what seems like an obvious connection between concepts to you as an expert may not be so obvious to your students. It is much more difficult for novice learners to find connections that experts easily see because we often take what we know for granted and think that others share our knowledge base. We need to remind ourselves often that new learners do not yet possess a robust knowledge base. When you remind students of related content and draw attention to connections between concepts, it's a great opportunity to put the previously learned content front and center. This makes it easier for students to take in the new material.

Mini Lesson on Reading Strategies

Teaching students how to build some background knowledge prior to reading is another effective strategy. Reading is one of the primary ways students learn content, yet many students report spending hours on this task without always walking away with an understanding of the content.

This is in part because of a lack of prior knowledge on the subject matter. Two incredibly simple yet powerful tools in textbooks are the table of contents and chapter summaries. Unfortunately, these features are often overlooked by students. Reading the table of contents provides students with a basic overview of the content addressed in the chapters. The organizational structure of information in the table of contents will undoubtedly help students take in and store information more efficiently. It provides students with the organizational schema for the content. Reading the chapter summary before starting to read the chapter will also assist students with building a base of knowledge on the subject matter. This is particularly important in introductory courses or courses where students often do not have much content knowledge about the subject. The brief chapter summary is a great way to begin to learn the content before diving into the details of the chapter. If the information in the summary is familiar, reading it activates prior knowledge. If the chapter summary information is completely new, this activity serves to create a basic knowledge base, thus making it easier for students to take in and process the chapter content. To help students understand the value of this activity, tell them how they are more likely to understand a movie if they saw the trailer before watching the movie. In other words, the trailer provides some background information on the movie plot that makes it easier to understand the plot when watching the movie.

Mini Lessons Prior to Assigning a Reading

As faculty, we often ask students to read something before we lecture on the content because we want students to come to class with some background knowledge so they can actively participate in discussions and answer questions. This is particularly true for those who are using the discussion-based lecture format. Unfortunately, students often don't do the reading before class (Burchfield & Sappington, 2000). This failure to complete assigned readings may be caused by factors such as poor time management or motivation. Also, previously students may have not found reading to be a good investment of their time. In other words, students may have spent hours reading only to be frustrated with how little they understand afterward, most likely when taking courses on material that is brand new to them. As we learned from the Recht and Leslie (1988) study, the lack of prior knowledge makes it difficult to learn from reading. A very simple strategy we can use as faculty to combat this is to provide students with some background information before asking them to read a chapter. Giving a brief preview lecture, highlighting some of the important concepts, and reviewing challenging terminology or content before assigning the reading can help students gain more from the time they spend reading. These mini lectures can be during the last 5 to 10 minutes of class. This approach serves as a preview of the content for the next chapter. Again, this strategy is designed to develop or build background knowledge so that it will be easier for students to make connections and take in the new content when reading. The combination of the mini lecture and the increased likelihood that they will be learning more from reading the chapter increases the likelihood that they will have some background knowledge before you begin your main lecture on that content. This approach requires us to rethink the way we lecture. A mini lecture preview of the chapter is followed by the reading assignment, which is followed by the in-depth lecture. It's a win-win for all.

SUMMARY

There are many effective strategies to help students use prior knowledge to more effectively and efficiently learn new information presented during a lecture. These strategies assist with learning new information and also allow students to practice recalling the information, which as we will see in Chapter 8, is also beneficial to the learning process. Finally, it is critical to note that many of the strategies noted need not take a great deal of class time.

REFERENCES

Atkinson, R. C., & Shiffrin, R. M. (1968). Human memory: A proposed system and its control processes. In K. W. Spence, & J. T. Spence, *The psychology of learning and motivation* (Vol. 2, pp. 89–195). New York, NY: Academic Press.

Baddeley, A. D. (2002). Is working memory still working? *European Psychologist, 7*(2), 85-97. doi:10.1027//1016-9040.7.2.85

Baddeley, A.D., & Hitch, G. J. (1974). Working memory. In G. A. Bower (Ed.), *Recent advances in learning and motivation* (pp. 47–90). New York, NY: Academic Press.

Baldwin, J. M. (1898). On selective thinking. *Psychological Review, 5*(1), 1–24.

Barr, R. B., & Tagg, J. (1995). From teaching to learning—a new paradigm for undergraduate education. *Change, 27*(6), 12.

Burchfield, C. M., & Sappington, J. (2000). Compliance with required reading assignments. *Teaching of Psychology, 27*(1), 58–61.

Cameron, G. T. (1993). Spreading activation and involvement: An empirical test of a cognitive model of involvement. *Journalism Quarterly, 70*, 854–867.

Goswami, U. (2008). Principles of learning, implications for teaching: A cognitive neuroscience perspective. *Journal of Philosophy of Education, 42*, 381–399.

Heit, E. (1994). Models of the effects of prior knowledge on category learning. *Journal of Experimental Psychology: Learning, Memory, and Cognition, 20*, 1264–1282. doi:10.1037/0278-7393.20.6.1264

James, W. (1890). *The principles of psychology*. New York, NY: Holt.

Littlemore, J. (2001). The use of metaphor in university lectures and the problems that it causes for overseas students. *Teaching in Higher Education, 6*, 333–349. doi:10.1080/13562510120061205

Miller, G. A. (1956). The magical number seven, plus or minus two: Some limits on our capacity for processing information. *Psychological Review, 63*, 81–97.

Recht, D. R., & Leslie, L. (1988). Effect of prior knowledge on good and poor readers' memory of text. *Journal of Educational Psychology, 80*, 16–20. doi:10.1037/00220663.80.1.16

Schwartz, B. L., Son, L., K., Kornell, N., & Finn, B. (2011). Four principles of memory improvement: A guide to improving learning efficiency. *International Journal of Creativity and Problem-Solving, 21*, 7–15.

Snyder, J. S., Holder, W. T., Weintraub, D. M., Carter, O. L., & Alain, C. (2009). Effects of prior stimulus and prior perception on neural correlates of auditory stream segregation. *Psychophysiology, 46*, 1208-1215. doi:10.1111/j.1469-8986.2009.00870.x

Sterner, P., & Wedman, J. (1996). *The influence of prior experience and process utilization in solving complex problems*. Retrieved from ERIC database. (ED400275)

Unsworth, N. (2016). Working memory capacity and recall from long-term memory: Examining the influences of encoding strategies, study time allocation, search efficiency, and monitoring abilities. *Journal of Experimental Psychology: Learning, Memory, and Cognition, 42*, 50–61. doi:10.1037/xlm0000148

van Kesteren, M. R., Rijpkema, M., Ruiter, D. J., Morris, R. M., & Fernàndez, G. (2014). Building on prior knowledge: Schema-dependent encoding processes relate to academic performance. *Journal of Cognitive Neuroscience, 26*, 2250–2261. doi:10.1162/jocn_a_00630

Wetzels, S. J., Kester, L., van Merrienboer, J. G., & Broers, N. J. (2011). The influence of prior knowledge on the retrieval-directed function of note taking in prior knowledge activation. *British Journal of Educational Psychology, 81*, 274–291.

Willingham, D. T. (2009). *Why don't students like school? A cognitive scientist answers questions about how the mind works and what it means for the classroom*. San Francisco, CA: Jossey-Bass.

Woolfolk, A. (2013). *Educational psychology* (12th ed.). Boston, MA: Pearson Education.

4

CAPTURING ATTENTION AND EMPHASIZING IMPORTANT POINTS

In addition to activating prior knowledge, capturing attention is also essential for learning. As we discussed in Chapter 3, what we attend to has a significant impact on the memory process. Think back to the three main components involved in memory: sensory memory, working memory, and long-term memory. When we pay attention to information, we are giving information a chance to pass through our sensory memory and move into our working memory. Without attending to the information in some way, learning is not possible; you cannot remember what you never perceived. Attention is needed during the working memory stage as well. Although it is possible to take in information effortlessly or without the intention to do so, we are much more likely to remember content when we attend to the information in a purposeful way (Woolfolk, 2013). Attention is therefore an important first step in the learning process, and student attention is particularly important during lectures.

Gaining and maintaining a person's attention are challenging because many other stimuli are constantly competing for attention. While sitting in a lecture, a student's attention may shift in many ways—daydreaming, looking out a window at a beautiful summer day, or looking at a website on a laptop. Mobile technologies have made it even more difficult for faculty to maintain students' attention. During class, students have easy access to social media on their phones, laptops, and other mobile devices. With everything that is happening in the world, it is very easy for students to become distracted during class, check in on social media, send a text, or engage in some other media-related task that is not connected to the course content. Of course, it is not just students who become distracted.

When you look around at department meetings, conference sessions, or even lunch with colleagues, it is obvious that many faculty members are often also checking their phones. Not surprisingly, students today report multitasking more frequently than students from previous generations (Carrier et al., 2009). Unfortunately, these multitasking behaviors that shift attention away from the lecture have a negative impact on learning (Junco, 2012; Wood et al., 2012). Researchers have found that this negative impact extends beyond the multitasker and has adverse effects on classmates as well. This was illustrated in an experimental study conducted by End, Worthman, Mathews, and Wetterau (2010). In this study, a confederate's phone rang for five seconds while participants viewed a recorded presentation. Students missed essential content in their notes when the phone rang during the time that tested material was presented in the lecture. More specifically, students in the class with the ringing cell phone correctly included key material in their notes about 48% of the time, compared to about 81% for the control group with no phone ringing. The phone ringing significantly reduced the likelihood of capturing specific material in notes during the lecture. This also translated into poorer performance. Sixty-nine percent of students in the cell phone ringing group responded correctly to a test question, whereas 95% of students in the no cell phone group responded correctly to this same test question (End et al., 2010).

In another study, this one conducted by Sana, Weston, and Cepeda (2013), it was found that the non-course-related use of a laptop during class had a negative effect on the academic performance of the student who used the laptop for a reason not related to the class and on the performance of nearby classmates. Interestingly, students in this study reported that the multitasking of other students did not negatively influence their own learning, which turned out to be incorrect (Sana et al., 2013). Thus, students may not even be aware of how easily their attention can drift and the negative consequences that occur as a result of reduced or lost attention. Given the significance of these findings, it is important to establish a classroom culture where learning is the focus, and distractions from cell phones, tablets, and other technology tools for purposes other than for learning are kept to a minimum. Reducing multitasking behaviors increases the likelihood that students will attend to course-related content. To accomplish this incredibly challenging task, we need to establish classroom policies that minimize distractions, emphasize the importance of a learning-focused classroom culture on the first day of class, and maintain this environment throughout the semester by addressing behaviors that can have a negative impact on learning.

Individuals are most likely to focus their attention when they have high interest in the content being discussed. This is true for everyone, including students sitting in a college classroom. Students will come to class with varying levels of interest in the subject matter. Some students may be fascinated with course content, while others may not be interested much, if at all, in the subject matter. Unfortunately, overall interest is often lower in required general education courses because students take the course to fulfill a requirement rather than because of interest. Helping students see the value and meaning of the course and how it connects to their everyday life may increase their attention, motivation, and ultimately their learning. To this end, we can explicitly communicate the value of the course content to our students. For example, you could share the research on the positive consequences of taking liberal arts courses. In a study conducted by Seifert and colleagues (2008), results revealed that participating in liberal arts course work had several benefits, including higher levels of overall well-being, development of leadership skills, increased intercultural effectiveness, and a stronger desire to engage in learning. Informing students of these positive outcomes and clearly demonstrating how these skills are highly valued in the world of work can increase attention and motivation. Being interested in the subject matter is also important when students are completing required reading. In a study conducted by Fulmer, D'Mello, Strain, and Graesser (2015), students reported less mind wandering when reading about content that interested them. Thus, it is important for faculty to find a way to spark student interest and highlight the value of the course content in lectures and readings.

Difficulty level also plays a role in whether students will exert effort to pay attention during the lecture. Research shows that students are most likely to pay attention and cognitively engage with academic tasks when the task is of moderate difficulty (Gickling & Armstrong, 1978). When presented with content that is too easy, students will quickly get bored and attention will drift. When presented with content that is perceived to be too challenging, students are more likely to disengage and shift their attention from the task at hand because they don't believe they can successfully learn the content (Lynch, Patten, & Hennessy, 2013). In other words, low self-efficacy for the task can result in lower levels of attention. This is where scaffolding comes into play. Vygotsky (1962), a developmental psychologist, noted the important role teachers, adults, or peers play in helping others learn. Specifically, he demonstrated how supports provided by teachers serve as a scaffold for the learner, making it much more likely for students to experience success at learning the content or skill (Woolfolk, 2013). If a student is sitting in a lecture and consistently hears unfamiliar vocabulary and concepts, it is likely this student will become frustrated and stop paying attention. However, with scaffolding, complex concepts are broken down into simpler, more accessible concepts; meaningful examples are used; and students are more likely to pay attention and ultimately learn the content. Students will exert more effort at maintaining their attention when they believe it is important and when they believe that exerting this mental energy on the task will lead to productive outcomes.

The delivery of the course content is also connected to student attention. Many students report being bored during lectures, especially when lectures involve copying notes from slides (Mann & Robinson, 2009). During monotone, boring lectures, student attention drops quickly. When this happens, students are more likely to turn to social media and engage in off-task behaviors (Flanigan, & Babchuk, 2015). As noted earlier, being off task negatively affects the learning process. Although education is not the entertainment industry, and professors are not performers, it is important for us to approach our lectures with a sense of passion for our discipline. Our enthusiasm and positive energy can be contagious and assist with gaining and maintaining student attention (Patrick, Hisley, & Kempler, 2000). This can be explained in part by the social contagion model of motivation in which students will be more interested and engaged in learning tasks when they perceive their professors to be intrinsically motivated to teach the content. In other words, the internal motivation is contagious and spreads to the students. Research has supported this model; for example, Radel, Sarrazin, Legrain, and Wild (2010) found that students reported higher levels of interest and enjoyment for the learning task when they believed the professor was intrinsically motivated.

Even when professors are charismatic and engaging, maintaining high levels of attention for long periods of time is a challenge. Researchers have found some evidence for attentional drift patterns during lectures. Johnstone and Percival (1976), for instance, found that inattention levels were high at the beginning of class and then peaked again at about 10 to 18 minutes into the lecture. Risko and colleagues (2012) found that higher levels of mind wandering were reported by students during the second half of a one-hour class (49%) compared to the first half of class (30%). Similarly, Farley, Risko, and Kingstone (2013) found that student levels of attention continued to decrease after every 5-minute block of a 40-minute lecture. This is particularly problematic as lecture content presented during the second half of a lecture is often more difficult to understand. Professors often shift from simple to complex content during a lecture; as a result, attention is drifting just when it is needed the most.

There are ways to help students maintain attention throughout a class period. Incorporating lecture pauses where active learning strategies are used helps to maintain student attention. So the next question is, how long should lecture segments be before introducing an active learning pause? It is likely you have heard that lectures shouldn't be longer than 15 to 20 minutes. Actually, although this is a common faculty belief, very little research supports it. In a study investigating attention and concentration during a lecture, Burns found that attention dropped to a low point after 15 to 20 minutes (as cited in Burke & Ray, 2008). However, the amount of time students pay attention varies dramatically depending on many factors such as their interest in the subject matter, the effectiveness of the lecturer, and students' level of fatigue. In a research study that involved observing 90 first-year chemistry lectures, Johnstone and Percival (1976) found that attentional drifts varied significantly among students from lecture to lecture and from lecturer to lecturer.

Similarly, many faculty members believe that learning will be decreased if class periods are too long (Davidson, 1984). However, the length of the class period does not seem to be the most important variable. Fike and Fike (2013), for example, compared longer and shorter mathematics classes and found that class length was not a significant predictor of academic performance. Some researchers have even found that students perform better in longer class sections once a week than shorter sessions twice a week (Gupta, Harris, Carrier, & Caron, 2006). Thus, which teaching methods are being used seems to matter much more than the duration of the lecture or class period.

However, even with limited research on the importance of lecture length, we know that attention will wander when we receive what we believe to be repetitive information for a period of time (Mooncyham & Schooler, 2016). The human brain is simply not wired to listen to a lecture that goes on forever. Therefore, breaking up lectures into segments, using brief active learning exercises in between the segments, is good pedagogical practice (Mazur, 1997). Although there is nothing magical about the 15- to 20-minute time period, it can serve as a good metric as long as we remember that time on task is not necessarily the most important variable we should consider when determining the length of a lecture segment. The content and how this content is being delivered are more important. Research over a long period of time has supported using active learning breaks after lecture segments (Hake, 1997). Researchers found that using an interactive technique such as questioning after 15-minute lecture segments helped students maintain their attention throughout the entire class period (Burke & Ray, 2008). To maximize attention, it is important for us to communicate our content in passionate, effective lecture segments followed by brief active learning opportunities. This approach increases the likelihood of students learning your course content.

Because it is normal for attention to drift, it is critical to have the students' attention before presenting any important content. As noted previously, attention is needed to take in new information. Using attention-grabbing activities has been found to increase learning. Rosegard and Wilson (2013) found that using a 90-second attention-grabbing activity such as a poem or puzzle related to course content increased student learning for the lecture that followed. Directing student attention to the big ideas of lectures helps students focus on what is most important and is a standard strategy used in TED talks. Identifying the most important points in a lecture is often one of the most challenging tasks facing an undergraduate. With limited background knowledge in the subject matter it is very difficult for the learner to discern what information holds the most value.

When developing a lecture and class activities, it is important to keep in mind that experts and novices process information very differently. Hrepic, Zollman, and Rebello (2004) explored the differences in how experts and novices take in and decipher information. In their study, students and experts in the field watched a video and then answered questions about the video. Students performed much better on questions on content that was explicitly addressed multiple times. When the content was not reviewed in a comprehensive and repetitive manner, students attempted to make sense of the information but were often unsuccessful. In contrast, experts were able to use their background knowledge of the subject to make accurate inferences, increasing their understanding and performance without multiple exposures to the information. As discussed in Chapter 3, our background knowledge plays a powerful role in how we take in and use new information. Experts are in the fortunate position of having extensive background knowledge, whereas novice learners do not have this same luxury. Because new or novice learners don't have the necessary background knowledge to differentiate between the important and not-so-important content, they often spend more time and energy focused on details rather than the big ideas or major points (Hrepic et al., 2003). This can result in students failing to learn the essential information. A lack of understanding of primary concepts will also make it more difficult for students to learn additional content in a subject because it negatively affects their ability to see hierarchical and other relational connections between and among concepts.

The difficulty with differentiating between important and unimportant points is often illustrated by the notes students take during a class session. Many students attempt to write down everything a professor says, which results in a stream of notes without much organization and leaves the students with missing information. Sometimes the most important content is not captured. We can assist students with note-taking by including an organizational structure for our lecture, such as providing students with copies of our PowerPoint slides prior to class. Although this practice is beneficial to learners, some faculty are reluctant to provide slides before class for a variety of reasons. They may be concerned with attendance issues and whether providing slides will reduce note-taking behaviors. Bowman (2009) found no attendance differences in classes where PowerPoint slides were posted versus not posted. Babb and Ross (2009) looked at the timing of posting the slides and found that when slides were posted before class, attendance and participation were higher. In addition to attendance concerns, some faculty believe it is the student's responsibility to determine what is most important and that providing the notes works against this goal. Austin, Lee, and Carr (2004) found that students who were provided with *guided notes*, defined as slides consisting of about 80% to 90% content and 10% to 20% blank spaces for note-taking purposes, were not only able to capture the main points but also more likely to capture examples compared to students who were not provided with copies of the notes. This is very important because the student's notes from class serve as a primary resource for studying. Having the key content and relevant examples in their notes will most certainly help students learn the content. Thus, when we provide organizational tools such as access to our PowerPoint slides, concept maps, or outlines of material we are addressing during the lecture, we are increasing the likelihood of student learning. As their knowledge base increases, students will need less support and will be better able to extract the key points from a lecture, but in the beginning of the learning journey, students benefit from this instructor-provided support.

We see this same pattern in student reading. The lecture and the textbook are the two primary avenues for students to learn content in college, and processing information from each is relatively similar. Just as novice students have difficulty knowing what to write down during a lecture, novice readers have difficulty knowing which material in a book is most important. If you look at a textbook that has been highlighted by a student, you will often see almost everything highlighted or less important content highlighted more than the essential content. When students engage in ineffective highlighting practices, poor academic performance may result (Dunlosky et al., 2013; Gier-Kreiner, & Natz-Gonzalez, 2009). Although we can sometimes get frustrated when students engage in these ineffective highlighting strategies or when they have difficulty identifying the most important points from lectures, it is important for us to remember why this happens: Students don't know enough to differentiate the important from the unimportant. To combat this issue, we can teach students some effective strategies, such as how to build some background knowledge before reading a chapter or lecture, and we can also significantly help students by clearly emphasizing the most important points in our lectures and assigned readings.

These differences between experts and novices with respect to attention and understanding of new material cannot be overstated. It is very easy for us as experts to take our knowledge for granted and quickly frustrate our learners during a lecture. For students who are novices in the field, identifying what is most important while listening to a lecture is an incredibly challenging task, even though it may seem very easy or obvious to us. Thus, it is critical to continually assist students with differentiating the important from the less important. Explicitly informing students which content is of high value or importance will assist students in learning the content of our discipline. As students develop stronger foundational knowledge, they will be able to take on the task of identifying what is most important, but until then, we play an incredibly important role in helping students see the important concepts and organizational structure of our discipline.

LEARNING AND ENGAGEMENT STRATEGIES

Getting and holding attention is a critical aspect of learning. The following classroom strategies are designed to augment lectures by increasing student attention and assisting novice learners by emphasizing major points. These strategies may be completed as a method to break up lectures and often take only a few minutes of class time.

Creating a Classroom Culture Focused on Learning

Our actions before the semester even begins and during the first few class periods can have a significant impact on how much students pay attention and learn in the class. Because a learning-focused atmosphere is essential, a good first step in developing this type of environment is to develop a good rapport with students. Students are more likely to engage in learning-focused behaviors when they respect their professor and believe their professor cares about their learning. Some simple actions such as sending out a welcome e-mail prior to the start of the semester can be a productive start to developing a positive relationship with your students. Legg and Wilson (2009) demonstrated this in a study in which one group of students received a welcome e-mail prior to the start of the semester and the other group did not. In this experimental study, the professor did not know who received the e-mail because the mailing was managed by the teaching assistant. Results revealed that students who received the e-mail prior to the start of class had more positive impressions of the professor and the course at the beginning of the semester. Additionally, these more positive impressions were also evident at the end of the semester. This demonstrates how brief, simple interventions can be quite powerful.

On the first day of class, it's important to develop a learning-focused culture in the class. Classroom policies that promote learning and minimize distraction (i.e., not using cell phones or other technology for nonlearning purposes) are needed and must be clearly communicated, but how we communicate these policies matter. Syllabi that focus on negative behaviors and their consequences can send the message to your students that you are expecting them to engage in inappropriate behaviors and may not help you establish a good rapport with your students. Instead consider using a positive statement about how much you value a learning-focused environment and how you take your role in creating and maintaining a distraction-limited environment very seriously. Providing students with a rationale for the policies can promote a respectful relationship while also increasing the likelihood that students will follow the guidelines of the policy.

Address Off-Task Behaviors When They Occur

Even if you establish clear behavioral guidelines and provide your rationale for policies related to off-task behaviors in class, some students may still engage in behaviors that distract others. As faculty, it is our responsibility to address these off-task behaviors so all the students in our classes can focus their attention on the lecture content. Some very powerful, nonverbal strategies to address these behaviors include walking closer to the student who is engaged in off-task behavior and making eye contact with the student. Another strategy is to use the student's name in the context of the lecture. This is not the same as calling students out for their behavior. Instead of calling a student by name and telling him or her to stop the distracting behavior (an action that further distracts from learning), use the student's name when giving an example. For example, if John is off task, you might say something such as, "When John shared his experience with volunteering at his local elementary school, the scenario he described was a good example of operant conditioning." When the nonverbal and name-dropping approaches are not working, you may then need to verbally remind the student of the policy and ask him or her to stop engaging in the off-task behavior. Individual conversations with students outside the classroom may sometimes be needed, especially if a student is repeatedly engaging in disruptive classroom behaviors (Woolfolk, 2013).

Discuss the Detrimental Effects of Multitasking

Most students do not realize what a problem multitasking can be in the college classroom. Using phones, tablets, and computers for social purposes is a normal activity for most of us, and it can be challenging for students to turn off their devices when entering a classroom. Tell them about the research on how multitasking negatively affects learning and how their actions also have negative consequences for their classmates. Review with them the research on how important attention is to learning and how distractions such as cell phones and laptops can have a detrimental effect on their success and the success of their classmates (End et al., 2010; Sana et al., 2013). Engaging students in activities or discussions about studies such as these at the start of the semester can help students understand the importance of being on task and focused during a lecture. A few minutes of class time at the start of the semester can have a long-lasting, positive impact on the learning experience for all your students throughout the semester.

Identify the Big Ideas

Prior to each lecture, identify the three most important concepts, then develop a plan to emphasize these important points. One strategy is to write the big ideas on the board or put them in a PowerPoint slide so students know to look out for these concepts during the lecture. Some faculty might worry that by identifying just a few big ideas, they may be minimizing the importance of other content. Remember, though, that when students learn the important points, it will be easier for them to take in and digest the details because an organizational structure for the material is being created. Thus, providing students with assistance in determining the most important points will lead to more, not less, learning in the long run. During the lecture, we can inform students why we are using this strategy and how knowing the big ideas will serve as an information springboard for them to take in more detailed information during the lecture and reading. In other words, we can make them understand that the big ideas are a great start to learning the course content, but they are expected to dive much deeper into the content and learn more specific information as well.

One of the simplest strategies you can use to emphasize what is important is to simply tell them if it is important. Some faculty think it is the student's responsibility to decipher what is most important, but as discussed previously, this can be a very difficult task for novice learners. Why does it have to be a mystery? By making statements such as "This is important!" we can capture the attention of our students and help them know which topics demand more study time and energy. As students learn more about the discipline, they will be better equipped to identify the most important concepts without as much support.

Use a Hook or Attention Getter

Once you've identified the big ideas of your lecture, you'll want to think about how to grab students' attention before lecturing. As illustrated in the research study by Rosegard and Wilson (2013), using even a 90-second activity can help students refocus their attention on the lecture content. Hooks can vary based on content, or you can establish a cue that can be consistently used to emphasize the importance of a concept. Some examples of hooks could be an interesting image, question, story, or statistic communicated in a passionate way. Some examples of cues that important content is about to be discussed include straightforward language such as, "This is important" or "This is one of the big ideas," and making a visual gesture, using silence or a dramatic pause, or standing in a certain location in the room. In the beginning of the semester, you can explicitly describe these cues with your students, but as the semester progresses, this verbal explanation will no longer be necessary.

Be Passionate and Use Your Voice

Showing your passion about a subject matter is an excellent way to capture attention and is particularly easy if you are using a storytelling lecture or demonstration lecture. Students respond positively to professors who are excited about the course content (Patrick et al., 2000). Your enthusiasm about a topic can certainly communicate importance. Although you may naturally talk louder about content when you believe it is particularly exciting or important, consider developing a plan to use your voice to draw attention to the most important points. Change often grabs our attention, so talking more loudly or more softly will often capture the attention of your students. When a professor speaks with a monotone voice that doesn't change, students will likely get lost and have significant difficulty determining which concepts matter the most.

Use Gestures or Symbols

Another strategy to draw attention to major points during a lecture is to use gestures or symbols. There are a couple of different ways you can use gestures to emphasize importance. For instance, you may create a gesture such as waving your hands above your head that signifies importance. When you first use this gesture, explain to students that you will use it before presenting the big ideas. It works very much like saying "This is important" but is a nonverbal approach. You could also create gestures that directly connect to important concepts. With this approach, you would use different gestures for each big idea or important point. The use of the gesture itself signifies the content is important, and the act of using a gesture that relates to the content will assist students with remembering the important information. In essence, it serves as a retrieval cue, making it easier for students to extract information from long-term memory when it is needed. Another related strategy is the use of symbols. Similar to gestures, you could use a symbol that alerts the student that the content is important. A star next to a concept would be one example. Symbols that are consistently used for a given concept could also be used. For example, if a goal is to help students in an introductory psychology course to understand the many ways cognition applies to different theories, a ♦ symbol might be used. This symbol reminds students that it is a cognitive application of a given theory. The symbols may be simple or creative and might also be developed by students. Think about how well we know the simple icons on our smartphones. Attaching symbols or simple images to our important content will help students master the course content. Images are powerful learning tools (Mayer, 2009), and we discuss this in more depth in Chapter 5.

Build In Active-Learning Breaks

As discussed earlier, it is good pedagogical practice to break a large lecture into segments. Incorporating a brief active learning pause after each lecture segment can help students maintain attention and can increase their engagement and learning. The next chapter provides several activities you can use following lecture segments. However, it may be important to take a lecture break earlier than planned. One of the benefits of a live lecture is that you are constantly getting feedback from students. Most of this feedback will be nonverbal, yet this information can help you guide your lectures. In a study conducted by Farley and colleagues (2013), resarchers found that fidgeting was connected to lower levels of attention and learning. This means that when your students are fidgeting in their seats, their attention has probably drifted. It is therefore time to take action to get their attention back on track. You can do this by using one of your established attention grabbers or by taking a break from the lecture and using a brief active learning exercise. Thus, it may be important to have a few backup activities if additional lecture breaks are required.

Teach Students How to Read and Highlight Effectively

When students read the textbook prior to class, they can be better positioned to differentiate between the important and less important content in a lecture. However, this is only the case if the students understand what they read in the textbook. Unfortunately, students often fail to report a high level of understanding after reading a textbook chapter. One of students' most widely used strategies while reading is highlighting parts of the text, but most students are not effectively using this strategy. By teaching students a few basic tips on how to read and highlight more effectively, we can assist students with extracting key points from the text and lecture. As discussed in the previous chapter, teaching students to use textbook features such as the table of contents and chapter summaries can increase how much students learn from reading. Encouraging students to use the 3R (read-recite-review; McDaniel, Howard, & Einstein, 2009) or SQ3R (Survey! Question! Read! Recite! Review!) reading methods is advisable because they are supported by research (Artis, 2008; Carlston, 2011). When using the 3R method, students should first identify a manageable section of the chapter to read. Second, after reading it, they should close the book and make notes on that section (Harrington, 2016). It is critical for the book to be closed during the review stage because it forces students to actively engage with the content and use their own words to summarize what was learned rather than simply copying text from the book. Third, students reread the section and fill in their notes with any missing content. During this third step students can use their highlighters because they now possess some knowledge on the content and will be better able to identify the most important points. The SQ3R approach is the same as the 3R except for two additional steps: survey and question. Before reading, students are encouraged to preview the chapter so they have a sense of the type of content they will be learning. Next, students form questions about the chapter based on the preview and prior to reading the chapter. Some books have questions posed in the beginning of the chapter. In these cases students may think about these questions prior to reading. As students begin the reading process, they will be searching for answers to these questions. We can also provide questions about the readings to help students focus on the most important parts of the chapters. Encouraging students to only highlight one or two sentences from each paragraph or section also forces them to actively think about the content, determining what is most important. Teaching students some of these very simple, yet powerful reading strategies can help them learn course content.

SUMMARY

Students often report that lectures are boring and that it is difficult to learn from lectures. This often happens because an expert is attempting to inform novices, and at times novices do not understand the major point of the lecture and miss key information along the way. Learners in such situations have a difficult time determining what they should attend to at any given time and as a result get frustrated and lose interest. Helping learners to better process the information through effective reading to understand the big picture and the important components greatly assists the learning process. In addition, well-placed engagement activities at the appropriate places in the lecture based on the learning level of the students provide natural breaks and help them to maintain focus.

REFERENCES

Artis, A. B. (2008). Improving marketing students' reading comprehension with the SQ3R method. *Journal of Marketing Education, 30*, 130–137.

Austin, J. L., Lee, M., & Carr, J. P. (2004). The effects of guided notes on undergraduate students' recording of lecture content. *Journal of Instructional Psychology, 31*, 314–320.

Babb, K. A., & Ross, C. (2009). The timing of online lecture slide availability and its effect on attendance, participation, and exam performance. *Computers & Education*, 52, 868–881. doi:10.1016/j.compedu.2008.12.009

Bowman, L. L. (2009). Does posting PowerPoint presentations on WebCT affect class performance or attendance? *Journal of Instructional Psychology, 36*, 104–107.

Burke, L. A., & Ray, R. (2008). Re-setting the concentration levels of students in higher education: An exploratory study. *Teaching in Higher Education, 13*, 571–582.

Carlston, D. L. (2011). Benefits of student-generated note packets: A preliminary investigation of SQ3R implementation. *Teaching of Psychology, 38*, 142–146.

Carrier, L. M., Cheever, N. A., Rosen, L. D., Benitez, S., & Chang, J. (2009). Multitasking across generations: Multitasking choices and difficulty ratings in three generations of Americans. *Computers in Human Behavior*, 25, 483–489. doi:10.1016/j.chb.2008.10.012

Davidson, M. S. (1984). *Report of the seventy-five minute task force*. Retrieved from ERIC database. (ED253152)

Dunlosky, J., Rawson, K. A., Marsh, E. J., Nathan, M. J., & Willingham, D. T. (2013). Improving students' learning with effective learning techniques: Promising directions from cognitive and educational psychology. *Psychological Science in the Public Interest, 14*(1), 4–58. doi:10.1177/1529100612453266

End, C. M., Worthman, S., Mathews, M. B., & Wetterau, K. (2010). Costly cell phones: The impact of cell phone rings on academic performance. *Teaching of Psychology, 37*, 55–57. doi:10.1080/00986280903425912

Farley, J., Risko, E. F., & Kingstone, A. (2013). Everyday attention and lecture retention: The effects of time, fidgeting, and mind wandering. *Frontiers in Psychology, 4*, 1–9.

Fike, D. S., & Fike, R. (2013). A multilevel analysis of the association of class schedule with student outcomes in community college developmental math. *Community College Journal of Research and Practice, 37*, 816–827.

Flanigan, A. E., & Babchuk, W. A. (2015). Social media as academic quicksand: A phenomenological study of student experiences in and out of the classroom. *Learning and Individual Differences, 44*, 40–45. doi:10.1016/j.lindif.2015.11.003

Fulmer, S. M., D'Mello, S. K., Strain, A., & Graesser, A. C. (2015). Interest-based text preference moderates the effect of text difficulty on engagement and learning. *Contemporary Educational Psychology, 41*, 98–110. doi:10.1016/j.cedpsych.2014.12.005

Gickling, E. E., & Armstrong, D. L. (1978). Levels of instructional difficulty as related to on-task behavior, task completion, and comprehension. *Journal of Learning Disabilities, 11*, 559–566. doi:10.1177/002221947801100905

Gier, V., Kreiner, D. S., & Natz-Gonzalez, A. (2009). Harmful effects of preexisting inappropriate highlighting on reading comprehension and metacognitive accuracy. *Journal of General Psychology, 136*, 287–300. doi:10.3200/GENP.136.3.287-302

Gupta, S., Harris, D. E., Carrier, N. M., & Caron, P. (2006). Predictors of student success in entry level undergraduate mathematics courses. *College Student Journal, 40*(1), 97–108.

Hake, R. R. (1998). Interactive-engagement versus traditional methods: A six-thousand-student survey of mechanics test data for introductory physics courses. *American Journal of Physics, 66*(1), 64–74.

Harrington, C. (2016). *Student success in college: Doing what works!* (2nd ed.). Boston: MA: Cengage Learning.

Hrepic, Z., Zollman, D., & Rebello, S. (2004). Students' understanding and perceptions of the content of a lecture. *AIP Conference Proceedings, 720*, 189–192. doi:10.1063/1.1807286

Johnstone, A. H., & Percival, F. (1976). Attention breaks in lectures. *Education in Chemistry, 13*(2), 49–50.

Junco, R. (2012). In-class multitasking and academic performance. *Computers in Human Behavior, 28*, 2236–2243.

Legg, A. M., & Wilson, J. H. (2009). E-mail from professor enhances student motivation and attitudes. *Teaching of Psychology, 3*, 205-211. doi:10.1080/00986280902960034

Lynch, R., Patten, J. V., & Hennessy, J. (2013). The impact of task difficulty and performance scores on student engagement and progression. *Educational Research, 55*, 291–303. doi:10.1080/00131881.2013.825165

Mann, S., & Robinson, A. (2009). Boredom in the lecture theatre: An investigation into the contributors, moderators and outcomes of boredom amongst university students. *British Educational Research Journal, 35*, 243–258. doi:10.1080/01411920802042911

Mayer, R. E. (2009). *Multimedia learning* (2nd ed.). New York, NY: Cambridge University Press.

Mazur, E. (1997). *Peer instruction: A user's manual.* Upper Saddle River, NJ: Prentice Hall.

McDaniel, M., Howard, D., & Einstein, G. (2009). The read-recite-review study strategy: Effective and portable. *Psychological Science, 20*, 516–522. doi:10.1111/j.1467-9280.2009.02325.x

Mooneyham, B. W., & Schooler, J. W. (2016). Mind wandering minimizes mind numbing: Reducing semantic-satiation effects through absorptive lapses of attention. *Psychonomic Bulletin & Review, 23*, 1273–1279.

Patrick, B. C., Hisley, J., & Kempler, T. (2000). "What's everybody so excited about?": The effects of teacher enthusiasm on student intrinsic motivation and vitality. *Journal of Experimental Education, 68*, 217–236. doi:10.1080/00220970009600093

Radel, R., Sarrazin, P., Legrain, P., & Wild, T. C. (2010). Social contagion of motivation between teacher and student: Analyzing underlying processes. *Journal of Educational Psychology, 102*, 577–587. doi:10.1037/a0019051

Risko, E. F., Anderson, N., Sarwal, A., Engelhardt, M., & Kingstone, A. (2012). Everyday attention: Variation in mind wandering and memory in a lecture. *Applied Cognitive Psychology, 26*, 234–242. doi:10.1002/acp.1814

Rosegard, E., & Wilson, J. (2013). Capturing students' attention: An empirical study. *Journal of The Scholarship of Teaching and Learning, 13*(5), 1–20.

Sana, F., Weston, T., & Cepeda, N. J. (2013). Laptop multitasking hinders classroom learning for both users and nearby peers. *Computers and Education, 62*, 24–31.

Seifert, T., Goodman, K., Lindsay, N., Jorgensen, J., Wolniak, G., Pascarella, E., & Blaich, C. (2008). The effects of liberal arts experiences on liberal arts outcomes. *Research in Higher Education, 49*, 107–125. doi:10.1007/s11162-007-9070-7

Vygotsky, L. S. (1962). *Thought and action.* Cambridge, MA: MIT Press.

Wood, E., Zivcakavoa, L, Gentile, P, Archer, K., De Pasquale, D., & Nosko, A. (2012). Examining the impact of off-task multi-tasking with technology on real-time classroom learning. *Computers and Education, 58*, 365–374. doi:10/1016/j.compedu.2011.08.029

Woolfolk, A. (2013). *Educational psychology* (12th ed.). Boston, MA: Pearson Education.

5

EFFECTIVELY USING MULTIMEDIA AND TECHNOLOGY

EFFECTIVE LECTURERS SPEND MANY hours preparing the content of their presentations and also carefully thinking about how to clearly convey this content. Technology plays an important role in almost every aspect of our lives, and will not only continue to do so but also increase in prevalence. Learning is no exception. Research has shown that incorporating technology effectively into the learning process can increase student engagement and learning (Tang & Austin, 2009; Turney, Robinson, Lee, & Soutar, 2009). In the past, relatively few options were available with respect to the effective integration of technology into teaching and learning. Transparencies and filmstrips are two examples of early technology tools. Videotapes, disc players, and the ability to look up information on the Internet followed in later decades. In recent years, technology tools have grown exponentially, providing faculty with many ways to use multimedia to enhance the learning process. In fact, learning about all the various tools can be a monumental task, especially as new tools are being developed every day. Today, we can easily incorporate images, videos, virtual demonstrations, interactive polling, social media, and more into our lectures, and these enhancements range in cost from free to extremely expensive. Most students report they feel prepared to use technology effectively in college, with about half of the students reporting that the use of technology would increase their level of involvement in the class (Dahlstrom & Bischel, 2014).

However, the use of technology does not in itself enhance the learning process. In fact, there are many times when technology, in and out of the classroom, does more harm than good in terms of learning (Hashemzadeh & Wilson, 2007). For example, Mayer (2009) found that including too many bells and whistles in presentations reduced learning. There is no doubt that technology may sometimes be a distractor, moving student attention away from important course content. It is important to remember that technology is simply a tool, and it is our job as faculty to determine which tools will work best in our classrooms, given the skills of the instructor, the needs of the students, and the types of content to be learned. The focus needs to remain on the learning outcomes and how these outcomes can be best achieved. To accomplish this task, it is important to be familiar with the research literature on how multimedia tools affect the learning process.

MAYER'S MULTIMEDIA RESEARCH-BASED PRINCIPLES

Mayer (2009) is often cited as a leader in the field of multimedia learning. He has conducted numerous experimental studies on what works best and in which situations. By applying multimedia principles that are based on his significant research findings, learning can be enhanced. We discuss here the five principles most relevant to lecturing: multimedia, coherence, signaling, personalization, and modality (Mayer, 2009).

Multimedia Principle: Images Are Powerful Learning Tools

Visual images are powerful learning tools. Research has consistently demonstrated that meaningful visual images facilitate learning (Goswami, 2008; Mayer, 2009). Most individuals are able to process images much faster and more efficiently than they can process language (Seifert, 1997). Research supports the old saying that a picture is worth a thousand words. Once learned, we remember pictures more easily than words; this is called the *picture superiority effect* (Foos & Goolkasian, 2008; McBride & Dosher, 2002). Using images effectively in working memory has also been connected to positive learning outcomes (Unsworth, 2016).

The power of images is well illustrated in a study conducted by Mayer and colleagues (1996). College students with no prior knowledge of the content in the subject (meteorology) were randomly assigned to different learning conditions. Students who received a verbal and visual summary of the content outperformed students who only received a verbal summary. Holstead (2015) also found that students in a class where PowerPoint slides contained only images performed at higher levels (84%) compared to students in a class where text-based PowerPoint slides were used (76%). It is important to note that including visual images does not just give us a working-term memory boost but rather contributes to long-lasting memories (Schweppe, Eitel, & Rummer, 2015). There is a strong body of evidence demonstrating that adding a visual image to presented content significantly increases immediate and long-term learning.

Some researchers have investigated sequencing images and words. According to a review of the research conducted by Eitel and Scheiter (2015), findings are mixed on whether the image or words should be delivered first. However, complexity does have an impact on sequencing. As is similar for all learning, it appears that less complex information should be presented first followed by the more complex content. Mayer (2009) also found that it is important for the words and images that support the content to be close in proximity to one another.

Although instructor-provided images are quite effective, having students create or locate their own images related to the course content can be even more effective. Schmeck and colleagues (2014) found that students who created their own drawings while reading outperformed students who did not engage in drawing as well as students who received drawings from the instructor. This finding suggests it is important for the images to be not only relevant but also meaningful. When students create or find images connected to course content, it is very likely that the images selected will be relevant to their experiences. Having students self-select or create images is an excellent way to ensure that images are meaningful and relevant to students from diverse backgrounds. This approach increases the personal connection students have with the content, making learning more likely.

Coherence Principle: Less Is More

Perhaps one of the most frequent mistakes made when creating presentations is providing too much content on the slides. Although students may indicate a preference for slides that contain all the important information, slides with excessive content does not result in the highest levels of learning (Holstead, 2015). On the contrary, Mayer (2009) found that students learned more when there was less information on the slide. Likewise, students were also more likely to learn at a higher level when extraneous sounds, images, or animation were not included. These bells and whistles distracted learners. In other words, students learned best when slides were simple and focused only on essential information. Let us remember that presentation slides are called *visual aids* because they are supposed to be visual supports for learning; they are not intended to replace the lecture but rather enhance it. It is therefore not necessary or productive to capture all the lecture content on slides.

Signaling Principle: Emphasize Important Points

When using multimedia tools, it is important to use signaling techniques to draw attention to the most important content. Mayer (2009) found that learning increased when attention was focused on significant content. Thus, using bold or large fonts to emphasize a concept or an arrow to draw the eye to part of a chart can have a positive impact on learning. This is particularly important when presentations are delivered in an online format because the professor is not physically present and cannot point to a part of the slide. During live lectures, it is critical to draw students' attention to key parts of charts or other information contained on the slide, but it may be even more effective to do this by our actions rather than using arrows or other tools included in the multimedia software.

Personalization Principle: Keep It Conversational

Often, slides are filled with complex terminology or jargon and are presented in a very formal way. As already discussed, including too much content on slides can reduce learning. However, the nature of how we communicate the content matters too. Mayer (2009) found we learn better when simple, conversational language is used rather than complex, formal language. Using conversational pronouns such as "you" and "we" on slides can help us build a social connection with our students. Think about how we talk during conversations and use simpler language rather than more complex terminology. These more personal, simpler explanations can make it easier for students to take in and understand the content, which is particularly important when discussing complex content with novice learners. Bringing this conversational approach to our slides and lectures can have a positive impact on the learning process. For example, conversational language helps students feel more connected to us as faculty, whereas formal, complex language can add distance between us and our students. Research has shown that positive connections between professors and students have been linked to increased student achievement in addition to student learning (Wilson, Ryan, & Pugh, 2010).

Modality Principle: Be Quiet

One of the most common mistakes when lecturing with presentation slides is to talk while showing text-heavy slides. This is a learning challenge for students because they cannot listen to the words being spoken at the same time they are supposed to be reading the words on a slide. Verbal and written words are competing for the student's attention. In this situation, students struggle because they are trying to listen and read at the same time and are probably not very successful at doing either. Thus, student attention is divided, making learning less likely (Mayer, 2009). Savoy, Proctor, and Salvendy (2009) found that students were 15% less likely to recall verbal content when the professor used a presentation containing a significant amount of text compared to students who listened to the professor lecturing without having to read text on presentation slides. This research finding does not mean that abandoning the use of presentation slides altogether is the best solution. As previously indicated, slides that primarily consist of images can enhance the learning process.

MULTIMEDIA TOOLS

Although many different multimedia tools can be used to enhance learning, it is beyond the scope of this book to fully explore the technology tools available. The following is a review of a few of the most commonly used tools in the educational arena: PowerPoint and other presentation software, videos, polling tools, and social media.

PowerPoint and Other Presentation Software

PowerPoint and other presentation software are certainly the most used technology types in the college environment. Holstead (2015) found that 97% of students reported use of PowerPoint in most of their college classes. Some professors create their own PowerPoint presentations, whereas others rely on the PowerPoint slides included in the instructor resources that come from textbook publishers.

Student engagement when PowerPoint slides are being used varies significantly based on how the slides are being used. Research has shown that students have high levels of motivation and learning when professors use PowerPoint (Tang & Austin, 2009). This was illustrated in a study by Issa and colleagues (2011) in which medical students were assigned to learn content with typical slides that were fairly text heavy versus slides that were made using Mayer's (2009) research-based multimedia principles. Although the medical students in both groups showed gains between pre- and posttest scores, the students who were exposed to the slides that were designed according to research-based multimedia principles performed significantly better than students taught with more typical or traditional slides. Holstead (2015) also found that the nature of the slides mattered. In this study, students performed better when slides contained only relevant charts, graphs, or images compared to slides containing only text. Students in the images-only group rated the course and professor more favorably than did the students in the group that was shown bulleted lists on PowerPoint slides (Holstead, 2015). A surprising finding from this study was that students in the course where image-only slides were used indicated the course was easier than students in the course where bulleted PowerPoint presentations were used. Perhaps this was the case because students were better able to focus on what the professor was saying rather than being distracted by the text on slides. In other words, the images supported rather than detracted from learning, and the expert was the primary focus.

According to research, use of text-heavy PowerPoint slides is correlated with very low levels of engagement. Mann and Robinson (2009) found that students reported high levels of boredom when copying a great deal of text from PowerPoint slides. Mackiewicz (2008) found that student perceptions on the level of the effectiveness of PowerPoint were fairly consistent with the work of experts such as Mayer (2009), with students indicating that simpler, more visual slides are more effective than slides consisting primarily of text. Research suggests it is best to create slides with images that support the content, using limited text and no extraneous material or animation.

Because of significant exposure to ineffective slides, many faculty and students dislike the use of PowerPoint during lectures. Conferences and resources on the Internet include many presentations and videos on why PowerPoint should be avoided, with titles such as "Death by PowerPoint" (e.g., Eves & Davis, 2008) or "PowerPointless" (e.g., Anderson, 2009). As discussed by Isseks (2011), PowerPoint slides with a lot of text encourage mindless copying and do not offer a vehicle for high-level thinking and discussions. Too often, the focus is on the slides instead of the professor and the discussions. This is particularly true when the lights in the classroom are turned off, putting the slides on center stage and the professor in the background. This is not productive, a point highlighted by Harden (2007), who conducted a quasi-experimental study and found that the instructor, and not simply the presence of PowerPoint, was related to student learning.

Becoming familiar with the significant body of research on how to use tools such as presentation slides will help us strategically and effectively infuse technology into educational practices. When done well, presentation slides can enhance learning (Mayer, 2009).

Although PowerPoint is the most commonly used presentation tool, there are of course other presentation software options such as Prezi or Haiku Deck, both of which are Internet based. Prezi is often referred to as a visual storyboard. One primary advantage of this tool is the ability to zoom in on content and easily shift between main concepts and details. This can highlight the relationships and overall organization of the content. However, a disadvantage is that the motion on the screen during transitions may be distracting. Haiku Deck is another option that forces use of some of Mayer's (2009) multimedia principles by only allowing a few words and relevant photo images on each slide (Coget, 2015). With Haiku Deck, you create slides that are simple and visually effective. However, the restrictive format may not work for all your content. There is not much research investigating which specific presentation software works best under most conditions. Chou, Chang, and Lu (2015) found in an experimental study that using PowerPoint and Prezi led to similar academic achievement outcomes. The students in the PowerPoint and Prezi groups outperformed the control group where multimedia was not used. The most important factor is how well the professor lectures (Hardin, 2007), not the tool being used.

Regardless of which presentation tool you decide to use, it is advisable to make the slides available prior to class. Although many professors are concerned that this may have a negative effect on class attendance, research has not supported this concern. Babb and Ross (2009) found that attendance and participation were higher when slides were posted before class. Some faculty also worry that students won't take their own notes if the PowerPoint slides are provided prior to the lecture. Although it is true that students do not need to copy bulleted lists during the lecture, having a copy of the presentation slides in hand during class allows students to write down other important information such as examples and related content (Austin, Lee, & Carr, 1994). Also, unless the slides are read verbatim to students, which is a very poor practice, students will quickly discover that our slides are not a substitute for the lecture but rather an excellent organizational tool for note-taking during lectures. When our slides primarily consist of images, students will immediately see the need for note-taking during the lecture. Students report that they use the slides for note-taking purposes during class and as a study tool before exams (Holstead, 2015). Marsh and Sink (2010) found that students who had access to the slides during the lecture performed better on the final exam. Providing resources such as copies of the slides online can be particularly helpful to students with learning disabilities because it provides students with an organizational schema for the lecture.

Videos

Videos have long been used as a supportive tool for learning. Educators have used videos to take students on virtual field trips, bring experts to the classroom, and help students learn challenging content. How we bring videos to the classroom, however, has significantly changed in recent years. In the past, professors would often show full-length films, whereas today we are more likely to use short video clips. This change in the way we use videos is because of several factors. In the past, we had limited access to videos, thus we had fewer video options and were often only allotted one day to use the video. In recent years, online streaming of videos and YouTube clips has made access to video content easy, allowing short videos to be shown in class or as an assignment to be completed prior to the next class period. Attention spans have also influenced the length of video segments we use. According to Agarwal (2011), almost 90% of viewers will watch a 30-second video until the end, but only about 50% will do so when the video is two minutes long. The good news is that after this drop, it seems to level out with about 45% watching 5- to 10-minute videos until the end, and 40% watching entire videos that are 10- to 20-minutes. Less than 20% of viewers will watch videos that are an hour long. It is important to note that these statistics relate to online viewing of videos in general and are not necessarily connected to college learning experiences. College students will likely be more motivated to watch videos connected to course content, and faculty can increase their motivation by holding them accountable for doing so and ensuring the value of the video relative to the content being learning in the course.

Videos may be easily shown during a lecture to draw attention to a topic or to illustrate how the concept being studied affects individuals. In addition to illustrating a point being made during a lecture, in-class videos make outstanding conversation starters for small-group discussions. One of the main reasons for using videos is to increase student engagement. Students find videos engaging and enjoyable (Tang & Austin, 2009; Ventura & Onsman, 2009). The level of student engagement was significantly higher in classes where YouTube videos were used with 64% of students reporting being frequently or always engaged, compared to just under 30% reporting being frequently or always engaged in classes that did not include YouTube videos (Roodt, & Peier, 2013). Thus, incorporating videos into lectures is one way to increase student interest.

Another, perhaps even more important, reason for using videos is to improve learning. Videos are powerful tools that allow students to hear directly from experts, watch an experiment or demonstration, connect emotionally to content, and more. It is still important for faculty to set the stage for the video by directing students' attention to material that is related to the lecture and course learning outcomes and to give students an opportunity to reflect on what was learned from the video. Most students find YouTube videos a helpful addition to lectures, and learning levels have been found to be higher after students watched and discussed

YouTube videos (Fleck, Beckman, Sterns, & Hussey, 2014). For videos to have a positive impact on learning course material, they need to become a part of the plan. In other words, it takes a significant amount of time to find videos that support the learning objectives for the day and to determine the best pedagogical approach to incorporate the videos into the lecture.

If it is best for students to watch a video outside class time, asking students to complete a graded task such as a quiz or written assignment related to the video will increase the likelihood that students do in fact watch the video outside class. When showing a long video, it may be advisable to break it up into segments and have students digest the content in a discussion or written exercise before moving to the next segment. This may be helpful for videos shown in class or when students are viewing videos outside class. The nature of the video and the complexity of the content will obviously play an important role in determining how long segments should be to best facilitate learning the content.

Polling Tools

Among the several polling technology tools available, student response systems, or clickers, allow faculty to easily ask multiple-choice test questions during a lecture. Students use the response system to enter their answer and then the class responses are displayed visually on a graph or chart. With student response systems, faculty can link individual performance to an online grade book, or the tool can be strictly used for learning and not grading purposes. Research has shown that the use of clickers has been connected to increased learning (Campbell & Mayer, 2009; Lundeberg et al., 2011). This is not surprising. Clickers are engaging, and students receive immediate feedback about how well they are learning the content, which helps students more accurately monitor their learning progress and make adjustments to their study approaches as needed (Harrington, 2016). In addition, this feedback also guides the professor. If you discover that students are not understanding a concept, you can immediately review the concept again using different examples. This is much better than waiting for a quiz or exam to discover which concepts students are having difficulty grasping. The downside of the student response system is the potential cost. Some systems require the use of clickers, which have to be purchased by the student, department, or college.

Fortunately, several free polling systems are also options. Poll Everywhere and Kahoot! (a game-based approach to polling) are two examples. An Internet connection or cell signal is needed for both systems, and students are required to use their own mobile devices. Because access to technology has increased significantly in recent years, these options are being used more and more frequently. In a large-scale study of more than 75,000 college students, 86% reported owning a smartphone, and about half reported owning a tablet (Dahlstrom & Bichsel, 2014). As a result of increased access to mobile technology, faculty can easily incorporate technology into class activities without having to purchase or schedule the use of equipment. Despite this access to mobile technologies, only 6% of college students reported being encouraged to use their smartphones during class (Dahlstrom & Bischel, 2014); however, when mobile technology is used, students respond favorably. Shon and Smith (2011) conducted a course survey and noted more than 90% of students reported that Poll Everywhere was easy to use and helped them learn the content. In the game-based quizzing tool Kahoot!, high levels of engagement and learning have been found. In a study by Wang (2015), about 90% of students surveyed reported being engaged and motivated when using this polling tool, and about 75% reported that Kahoot helped them learn the content. Thus, the research investigating the value of these tools suggest that incorporating polling into lectures can increase student engagement, motivation, and learning.

Social Media

In 2005 only 12% of 18- to 29-year-olds were using social media, but today this number has grown to 90% (Perrin, 2015). Although the primary use of these tools continues to be in the social arena, more and more faculty are exploring the educational applications of these tools. For example, some professors are using Twitter in and out of the classroom. In large lecture courses, Twitter can be used as a way for students to ask each other questions and for faculty to better understand which concepts students are or are not grasping. During class, professors using Twitter can stop and take questions from the Twitter feed instead of students having to raise their hands. This approach may increase the likelihood of participation by students who may not be comfortable publicly asking a question (Pollard, 2014), which may be the case for students from different cultural backgrounds; shy, introverted students; and individuals afraid of making mistakes in front of others. The professor can also respond to other questions raised using Twitter after class if there is not enough time during class to address all questions. Thus, this approach can extend the classroom discussion beyond class time, encouraging students to engage with course content throughout the week. Most students (85%) who replied to a survey in a large course in which Twitter was used indicated that the use of Twitter was helpful (Pollard, 2014). Other online tools that allow for collaborative real-time participation, such as TodaysMeet, have also been connected to positive outcomes when used during lectures. In a study by Yates, Birks, Woods, and Hitchins (2015), students reported feeling more comfortable asking questions using these anonymous technology options and noted that these methods of asking questions didn't take lectures off track. Some students, such as those with learning challenges, may be hesitant to ask questions in front of their peers, so these anonymous options can increase the likelihood that students will ask their questions, which can obviously affect learning in a positive way.

Although social media has the potential to enhance lectures, it is important to note there are also challenges with this approach. For example, some students and faculty may wish to keep their personal and academic lives separate and may not be interested in using social media for educational purposes. One possible solution is to create two separate accounts, one for personal use and the other for academic use, but this of course requires regularly checking two separate accounts. In addition, we've already discussed the problems that arise when students multitask. When we ask students to take out their mobile devices and go to social media sites as an activity to augment a lecture, it may be very tempting for them to stay on these sites instead of refocusing their attention on the lecture. Overall, using social media has many potential benefits, but it is important to also be aware that social media may have detrimental effects on learning in and outside the classroom (Flanigan & Babchuk, 2015).

LEARNING AND ENGAGEMENT STRATEGIES

Careful integration of multimedia and technology has strong potential to augment lectures and increase learning opportunities for students. The following learning and engagement strategies are designed to provide examples of a variety of ways to enhance lectures by including images, videos, and other media components. If you already use some of these lecture enhancement strategies, think of ways to adapt them for future use.

Identify Relevant Images, Graphs, or Charts

In the previous chapter, we discussed the importance of identifying the big ideas of each lecture. Here, we recommend using images or videos that illustrate or expand on the biggest idea of each lecture. This can be a time-consuming process because it takes much effort and time to determine which images will work best and then even more time to find the images; however, this process is a valuable one. According to the research described earlier in this chapter (e.g., Schweppe, Eitel, & Rummer, 2015), using images will increase student learning and therefore is a worthwhile investment of your time. A good place to start is with materials provided by the textbook publisher. Often, publishers have copies of the images and graphs presented in the text ready for your use in presentation slides. You can also search the Web, looking for images that are open source documents. Cite where you find visual images to model the proper citation of images.

Create and Post Slides Prior to the Lecture

Start by choosing the presentation software (e.g., PowerPoint, Prezi, Haiku Deck) that will best augment the type of lecture you are using. If your campus has a teaching and learning center or instructional design team, contact the staff to evaluate the pros and cons of the different tools. Next, put the research conducted by Mayer (2009) into practice when creating your presentation slides, which means matching key words with images or other visual aids and then determining the best organizational structure for the slides. Tools such as Slide Sorter and Outline views in PowerPoint are helpful when looking at the overall organization of the slides. Avoid using too many words and excessive bells and whistles as these can reduce learning. Whenever possible, use conversational, simple language. Slide backgrounds should be consistent and simple and not distract from the slide content. Some backgrounds make it very difficult to read the text, and the choice of font can also play a role in learning, especially for students with reading disabilities. Rello and Baeza-Yates (2013) found that Helvetica, Courier, Arial, Verdana, and Computer Modern Unicode fonts increased readability for people with dyslexia. If you find that bulleted lists in PowerPoint are helpful to you as the presenter, create a separate file for your use when lecturing, or create an outline that contains the same content. There is nothing wrong with having notes for our lectures; in fact, this approach can enhance the organization of our teaching. However, it is important for us to realize that what is helpful to us may not be most helpful to our students. Thus, creating two versions, one for our organizational purposes and one that serves as an effective visual aid for students, is advisable. Posting our slides or other lecture materials prior to class provides students with an organizational schema for the content that will be discussed, which will help students take in the lecture content and better capture key concepts when taking notes.

Ask Students to Find Visual Images Related to Content

A good way for students to engage with the course content is for them to find an image or graphic that best captures the concept being learned. During an active learning break after a lecture segment or at the end of class, consider asking students to work with a partner or in small groups to create or find an image online that connects to the concepts just learned. If you use this method often, students will be creating an image-based study guide that will serve them well when preparing for exams. Note that images do not need to be complex. Simple drawings or images can also work very well. You can ask students to post images in a shared learning space in your course learning management system.

Use Video Clips to Emphasize Big Ideas

As discussed earlier, videos can increase student engagement and learning. Searching for video clips that effectively illustrate or connect to concepts in your course can be extremely time consuming, but it is a valuable activity. Start by using your resources. Textbook publishers often have many videos listed in the instructor resources materials that accompany the book. Your department or media services department may also have purchased video streaming services related to your discipline. It is also a great idea to consult with your colleagues on and off campus. Many disciplines have professional associations, many with a focus specific to teaching. If this is the case in your discipline, you may want to review the resources available on associations' websites or consult colleagues using an electronic mailing list or other means.

In terms of student resources, students may be asked to find a video clip related to the course reading for the next class period and e-mail the video link to the course instructor prior to class to illustrate a point to be made during the lecture. Asking to students work together to find a relevant video either before or during class works well, but it's important to recognize that this is a time-consuming process for students, too, and will likely be a more challenging task because they do not know the content as well as the instructor.

Once you've found the video clips, you have to decide how to best introduce and use them, either to set up the lecture or embed within the lecture. It's important for students to realize that the videos are a part of the lesson and not a break from it. You can increase attention and engagement during the video by first providing students with a list of questions they will be asked about the video. In addition, if students know they will discuss the video or answer questions after viewing it, this will help them stay on task during the video. Even a very brief two-minute video can easily take up 10 minutes or more of class time when these effective pedagogical practices are used, so be sure to plan appropriately.

Use Polling Technique

Polling is a great way to find out whether students are comprehending the lecture material. Students find polling to be an enjoyable experience that provides them with immediate feedback on how well they are learning the course content. You may want to include several polling questions for every big idea of the lecture. Before you begin this process, you may want to work with your teaching and learning center or instructional design team to determine which polling system will best meet your needs. You could also experiment with tools such as Poll Everywhere or Kahoot!. To integrate polling into your lecture, you will need to create the questions ahead of time and place them into your slide presentation. It is typically very easy to learn how to create the quizzes, but it is still important to become comfortable with how the software works. When you are first using the tool, you'll probably want to provide step-by-step directions to students on how to access it. Students can work with a partner if they do not have a smartphone or do not wish to use it for this purpose. Many faculty use polling questions after each big idea. If the results of the poll reveal that the class didn't understand the concept well, you will be able to revisit it before moving on the next topic. Because you can save the questions, it will be easy to use them again in an exam review or in a future lecture.

Consider Incorporating Social Media Into Lectures

At times, it might be more important for students to answer questions with short responses rather than with an objective multiple-choice test answer after a lecture segment. In these cases, you may want to consider tools such as Twitter or TodaysMeet so that students can reply to open-ended questions and their responses can be displayed anonymously. Ask students to share examples of a concept just discussed or identify the most important concept of the lecture. These tools can also be used as a vehicle for addressing student questions, which may be particularly important in large lecture classes where students are less likely to ask questions by raising their hand. Be prepared for the conversation to continue beyond the classroom. Students may continue to tweet questions or interact with classmates throughout the week. Decide how often you will be able to check the social media site and tell the students so their expectations are clear about your involvement outside class. As discussed previously, it is important to weigh the pros and cons of all technology. This approach does have the potential to encourage multitasking behaviors because you are sending students to social media. On the other hand, students will have access to the content outside class and can use it as a study tool.

Use Asynchronous Chats

If your institution uses a learning management system, you have a built-in feature that allows to you to moderate online discussions. Posting a critical-thinking question and requiring students to respond engages students with the course content in a way that is very different from a discussion during class. It provides students with an opportunity to read about and reflect on the content before responding. Some of the students who may be more resistant to speak out in class often contribute very thoughtful posts in this format. You might ask something similar to, "What one question would you have asked or comment would you have made during today's lecture if there were time for everyone to participate?" Themes brought up during online discussions can be incorporated into the lecture for the next class period and even included in class discussions.

SUMMARY

Many options are available for including multimedia and technology in lectures to enhance student experiences inside the classroom and to prepare for a class session. Images in PowerPoint presentations, technologies that allow for real-time collaboration in class, and videos all demonstrate positive outcomes with respect to student learning. At times, it is advantageous for students to identify the videos or images to be used in the course as a mechanism to increase their level of interest, engagement, and learning in the course.

REFERENCES

Agarwal, A. 2011. *What's the optimum length of an online video?* Retrieved from http://www.labnol.org/internet/optimumlength-of-video/18696/

Anderson, P. (2009). Powerpointless—or is it? *Training Journal*, Sept., 26–28.

Austin, J. L., Lee, M., & Carr, J. P. (2004). The effects of guided notes on undergraduate students' recording of lecture content. *Journal of Instructional Psychology, 31*, 314–320.

Babb, K. A., & Ross, C. (2009). The timing of online lecture slide availability and its effect on attendance, participation, and exam performance. *Computers & Education*, 52, 868–881. doi:10.1016/j.compedu.2008.12.009

Campbell, J., & Mayer, R. E. (2009). Questioning as an instructional method: Does it affect learning from lectures? *Applied Cognitive Psychology, 23*, 747–759. doi:10.1002/acp.1513

Chou, P., Chang, C., & Lu, P. (2015). Prezi versus PowerPoint: The effects of varied digital presentation tools on students' learning performance. *Computers & Education, 91*, 73–82. doi:10.1016/j.compedu.2015.10.020

Coget, J. (2015). Haiku Deck: A minimalist, high-impact alternative to PowerPoint. *Journal of Management Education, 39*, 422–427. doi:10.1177/1052562914540905

Dahlstrom, E., & Bichsel, J. (2014). *ECAR study of undergraduate students and information technology, 2014*. Retrieved from https://net.educause.edu/ir/library/pdf/ss14/ERS1406.pdf

Eitel, A., & Scheiter, K. (2015). Picture or text first? Explaining sequence effects when learning with pictures and text. *Educational Psychology Review, 27*, 153–180.

Eves, R. L., & Davis, L. E. (2008). Death by PowerPoint? *Journal of College Science Teaching, 37*(5), 8–9.

Flanigan, A. E., & Babchuk, W. A. (2015). Social media as academic quicksand: A phenomenological study of student experiences in and out of the classroom. *Learning and Individual Differences, 44*, 40–45. doi:10.1016/j.lindif.2015.11.003

Fleck, B. B., Beckman, L. M., Sterns, J. L., & Hussey, H. D. (2014). YouTube in the classroom: Helpful tips and student perceptions. *Journal of Effective Teaching, 14*(3), 21–37.

Foos, P. W., & Goolkasian, P. (2008). Presentation format effects in a levels-of-processing task. *Experimental Psychology, 55*, 215–227. doi:10.1027/1618-3169.55.4.215

Goswami, U. (2008). Principles of learning, implications for teaching: A cognitive neuroscience perspective. *Journal of Philosophy of Education, 42*, 381–399.

Hardin, E. E. (2007). Presentation software in the college classroom: Don't forget the instructor. *Teaching of Psychology, 34*, 53–57. doi:10.1080/00986280709336652

Harrington, C. (2016). *Student success in college: Doing what works!* (2nd ed.). Boston, MA: Cengage Learning.

Hashemzadeh, N., & Wilson, L. (2007). Teaching with the lights out: What do we really know about the impact of technology intensive instruction? *College Student Journal, 41*(3), 601–612.

Holstead, J. (2015). The impact of slide-construction in PowerPoint: Student performance and preferences in an upper-level human development course. *Scholarship of Teaching and Learning in Psychology, 1*, 337–348. doi:10.1037/stl0000046

Issa, N., Schuller, M., Santacaterina, S., Shapiro, M., Wang, E., Mayer, R. E., & DaRosa, D. A. (2011). Applying multimedia design principles enhances learning in medical education. *Medical Education, 45*, 818–826. doi:10.1111/j.1365-2923.2011.03988.x

Isseks, M. (2011). How PowerPoint is killing education. *Educational Leadership, 68*(5), 74–76.

Lundeberg, M. A., Kang, H., Wolter, B., delMas, R., Armstrong, N., Borsari, B., & . . . Herreid, C. F. (2011). Context matters: Increasing understanding with interactive clicker case studies. *Educational Technology Research and Development*, *59*, 645–671. doi:10.1007/s11423-010-9182-1

Mackiewicz, J. (2008). Comparing Powerpoint experts' and university students' opinions about Powerpoint presentations. *Journal of Technical Writing and Communication*, *38*, 149–165. doi:10.2190/TW.38.2.d

Mann, S., & Robinson, A. (2009). Boredom in the lecture theatre: An investigation into the contributors, moderators and outcomes of boredom amongst university students. *British Educational Research Journal*, *35*, 243–258. doi:10.1080/01411920802042911

Marsh, E. J., & Sink, H. E. (2010). Access to handouts of presentation slides during lecture: Consequences for learning. *Applied Cognitive Psychology*, *24*, 691–706. doi:10.1002/acp.1579

Mayer, R. E. (2009). *Multi-media learning* (2nd ed.). New York, NY: Cambridge University Press.

Mayer, R. E., Bove, W., Bryman, A., Mars, R., & Tapangco, L. (1996). When less is more: Meaningful learning from visual and verbal summaries of science textbook lessons. *Journal of Educational Psychology*, *88*, 64–73. doi:10.1037/0022-0663.88.1.64

McBride, D. M., & Dosher, B. A. (2002). A comparison of conscious and automatic memory processes for picture and word stimuli: A process dissociation analysis. *Consciousness and Cognition*, *11*, 423–460. doi:10.1016/S1053-8100(02)00007-7

Perrin, A., (2015). *Social media usage: 2005–2015*. Retrieved from http://www.pewinternet.org/2015/10/08/social-networking-usage-2005-2015/

Pollard, E. A. (2014). Tweeting on the backchannel of the jumbo-sized lecture hall: Maximizing collective learning in a World History survey. *History Teacher*, *47*, 329–354.

Rello, L. & Baeza-Yates, R. (2013). *Good fonts for dyslexia*. Proceedings of the 15th International ACM SIGACCESS Conference on Computers and Accessibility, Article No. 14. doi:10.1145/2513383.2513447

Roodt, S., & Peier, D. (2013). Using YouTube© in the classroom for the Net generation of students. *Issues in Informing Science and Information Technology*, *10*, 473–488.

Savoy, A., Proctor, R. W., & Salvendy, G. (2009). Information retention from PowerPoint™ and traditional lectures. *Computers & Education*, *52*, 858–867. doi:10.1016/j.compedu.2008.12.005

Schmeck, A., Mayer, R. E., Opfermann, M., Pfeiffer, V., & Leutner, D. (2014). Drawing pictures during learning from scientific text: Testing the generative drawing effect and the prognostic drawing effect. *Contemporary Educational Psychology*, *39*, 275–286. doi:10.1016/j.cedpsych.2014.07.003

Schweppe, J., Eitel, A., & Rummer, R. (2015). The multimedia effect and its stability over time. *Learning and Instruction*, *38*, 24–33. doi:10.1016/j.learninstruc.2015.03.001

Shon, H., & Smith, L. (2011). A review of Poll Everywhere audience response system. *Journal of Technology in Human Services*, 29, 236–245. doi:10.1080/15228835.2011.616475

Siefert, L. S. (1997). Activating representations in permanent memory: Different benefits for pictures and words. *Journal of Experimental Psychology: Learning, Memory, and Cognition*, 23, 1106-1121. doi:10.1037/0278-7393.23.5.1106

Tang, T. L., & Austin, M. J. (2009). Students' perceptions of teaching technologies, application of technologies, and academic performance. *Computers & Education*, 53, 1241–1255. doi:10.1016/j.compedu.2009.06.007

Turney, C. M., Robinson, D., Lee, M., & Soutar, A. (2009). Using technology to direct learning in higher education: The way forward? *Active Learning in Higher Education*, *10*(1), 71–83.

Unsworth, N. (2016). Working memory capacity and recall from long-term memory: Examining the influences of encoding strategies, study time allocation, search efficiency, and monitoring abilities. *Journal of Experimental Psychology: Learning, Memory, And Cognition*, 42, 50–61. doi:10.1037/xlm0000148

Ventura, S., & Onsman, A. (2009). The use of popular movies during lectures to aid the teaching and learning of undergraduate pharmacology. *Medical Teacher*, 31, 662–664. doi:10.1080/01421590802641489

Wang, A. I. (2015). The wear out effect of a game-based student response system. *Computers & Education*, 82, 217–227. doi:10.1016/j.compedu.2014.11.004

Wilson, J. H., Ryan, R. G., & Pugh, J. L. (2010). Professor-student rapport scale predicts student outcomes. *Teaching of Psychology*, 37, 246–251. doi:10.1080/00986283.2010.510976

Yates, K., Birks, M., Woods, C., & Hitchins, M. (2015). #Learning: The use of back channel technology in multi-campus nursing education. *Nurse Education Today*, 35, e65–e69. doi:10.1016/j.nedt.2015.06.013

6

MAKING IT MEANINGFUL THROUGH EXAMPLES

EXAMPLES ARE POWERFUL LEARNING tools. Lee and Anderson (2012) point out that one of the primary ways to make lectures effective is to incorporate many examples. Based on what we know about how memory works, it makes sense that examples would help us remember. When learning new content, we naturally try to determine how this new information fits into our current knowledge base. In essence, we strive to put the new information into the context of what we already know.

It has long been known that new information is grafted onto previously learned information through a process of assimilation and accommodation (Baldwin, 1889; Piaget, 2001). Assimilation is a process by which new information is placed into categories similar to known information. When babies are introduced to a new object, they may quickly put it into their mouth to see if the object may be assimilated into the group of "things that can be eaten." If to that point everything presented to the child has been objects that provide nutrition, and this new item is a child's toy, such as a rattle, then this new object is accommodated by placing into a new category of "things that cannot be eaten." This process of assimilating items into existing categories and making accommodations by changing and creating new categories, when necessary, is a foundation for learning. It is also why it seems so natural to place things into categories: for example, introverts or extroverts, fast or slow, hot or cold, and friendly or mean. Gradations of categories certainly emerge through this process, but the first step is essentially dichotomous groupings.

Learning is a very active process. As we take in new information, we are constantly making comparisons to what is already known. This strengthens previously learned material, builds connections between previously learned information and new information, and makes new connections among and between concepts just introduced. Overall, examples are powerful learning aids as they help us make these connections to prior knowledge and assist us with seeing connections between new concepts, building and strengthening our neural pathways.

When we use examples, we are tapping into a memory concept called *elaboration*, the act of adding to information being learned by identifying relevant experiences and examples. One particularly effective type of elaboration is called *relational elaboration*, which occurs when we compare and contrast features of the new information being learned with the features of other concepts we have previously learned. As professors, we naturally use this technique when lecturing. For instance, after introducing a new topic, we often discuss how this topic relates to a previously discussed topic, reviewing similarities and differences. Students are taught this process when they are asked to compare and contrast two concepts, theories, or processes on examinations and in papers. Comparing and contrasting theories and other content is also a typical lecture activity to teach new concepts and to model how experts think about new information. Not surprisingly, there is a strong connection between taking a deeper look at how concepts relate and how well we learn the content (Hamilton, 1997).

When we attach meaning to concepts by using relevant examples, we are also increasing student motivation to learn the content. Motivation plays an important role in learning. Research has shown that that high levels of motivation are associated with high levels of achievement (Walker, Greene, & Mansell, 2006; Waschull, 2005), probably because motivated students are more likely to pay attention and exert high levels of effort (Goodman et al., 2011). Enhancing meaning through real-world applications is a primary way to increase motivation for learning (Wlodkowski & Ginsberg, 1995). By highlighting the importance of our content through meaningful, real-world examples and scenarios that are relatable to our students, we can have a positive impact on student motivation and learning.

Using examples from everyday life is an excellent method to pave the way for high levels of learning as well as increase long-term retention of information. When we use examples from everyday life, our students are able to easily connect new content to familiar experiences, situations, or knowledge. Connecting material to our selves, called the *self-reference effect*, is a natural and efficient learning system (Rogers, Kuiper, & Kirker, 1977). This form of elaboration is powerful because our memory for the familiar is much stronger than our memory for the unfamiliar (Wood et al., 1999), and what could be more familiar than our own lives? In some disciplines, such as psychology, it is easy to identify everyday examples that naturally fit into course content. For instance, when teaching the concept of negative reinforcement, which is the increase of a specific response as the result of the removal of an aversive stimulus, many psychology professors use seatbelts as an example. Although the concept alone might be difficult for most individuals to remember, it is much easier if an example that is relevant and grounded on previously known information is provided. If people do not put on their seatbelt, cars are manufactured to emit an irritating series of beeps or a buzzing sound to indicate the seatbelt is not secured. The removal of the irritating sound (aversive stimulus) when you buckle your seatbelt increases the likelihood that you will continue to use your seatbelt in the future (specific response). As most students have had this experience before, they can relate to it. This new concept, negative reinforcement, is then linked to a familiar experience, seatbelt use. This connection makes it much more likely that the content will move from working memory to long-term memory.

In addition to helping students encode this new information, the neural connections being established also assist students with accessing or retrieving this information when it is needed in the future. Thus, examples help students encode information more effectively and make the retrieval process easier. To be as effective as possible, however, it is important for students to be able to relate to the examples. This is facilitated by getting to know your students so you can better identify examples that are personally and culturally relevant. If you are teaching a course with students who don't drive or travel by car often, the example just described would not be meaningful and therefore be of little value. In such cases, the example is actually detrimental as it is additional irrelevant information, which will make learning more difficult. Although the connection between course content and everyday life might be more apparent in some disciplines than others, it is typically possible to find everyday examples that connect to one's discipline, content, and student experiences. In addition to personal examples, we can also turn to pop culture or current events. When students are familiar with an example from pop culture or current events, the content comes alive and gives immediate meaning to the concepts. If students are not familiar with the pop culture reference or current event, confusion can result. Thus, it is probably best to describe the scenario in detail or even show a brief related video clip so that the example has value to your students. As said before, knowing your students will make this process of finding relevant examples much easier.

Not all examples need to rely on personally familiar content. Rather than connecting to personal experiences or current events, some examples simply provide an additional explanation or demonstration of a concept being learned. This type of example is also very powerful. For instance, in a public speaking course, the professor might provide students with several examples of effective or ineffective speeches. The students do not have to be already familiar with the speeches for this teaching technique to be helpful. The examples work because they provide additional information about the concept being learned, helping students to more fully understand the concept. This approach is often used in health sciences, where many examples of healthy and unhealthy tissue samples may be presented. In art, this approach may be used to demonstrate subtle brush strokes of a certain painter.

In some cases, a verbal explanation of the example will be effective; however, as noted in Chapter 5, examples are often much more powerful if a visual component is included. This is particularly effective in disciplines that are very visual in nature (e.g., math or art). Simple strategies such as using the whiteboard can sometimes add the visual dimension needed, but we may also want to look to technology for additional ways to make the most of examples. Technology allows us to bring powerful examples to our classes that may have not been possible otherwise. Videos, images, and sounds can add clarity to concepts already explained or may be used to introduce new examples of the concepts. Videos can be particularly helpful when we want to share examples that are complex in nature, when limited resources or physical space restraints prohibit us from showing the example or conducting the demonstration in the classroom, and when actual exposure may be hazardous. A historical example, for instance, could be discussed, but showing a video of the example would likely enhance the student learning experience. Other technology tools might include websites, document cameras, or educational apps. All these tools allow us to easily bring examples from around the world into our classroom.

MODELING

Modeling is an effective way for us to help students learn by example during lectures. The process of modeling is essentially acting out an example. Some disciplines rely heavily on this lecturing technique. Can you imagine teaching students about mathematical concepts without illustrating how the concepts applied to different problems? Could you imagine a discussion on how to use lab equipment without the professor first demonstrating how to safely use the equipment or trying to teach students photography skills without demonstrating how to use different techniques? Modeling is an effective way for us to help students learn content because watching others is one of the primary ways we learn. This approach is called *observational learning* and has made valuable contributions to understanding human behavior for more than 50 years (Bandura & Walters, 1963). It is easier to carry out an action previously observed as it provides direct instruction on what and how to do something. This is why observation is such an important part of so many learning experiences. Although modeling may be a necessity in some disciplines, it is important in all areas. We can all think of ways we can use modeling to enhance learning.

Worked Examples and Demonstrations

Two types of modeling are worked examples and demonstrations. *Worked examples* are a type of modeling where the professor works through a problem or scenario. For instance, a business professor may show accounting students how to complete a ledger, or an education professor might show students how to complete a lesson plan before asking students to try it on their own in class or for homework. Students learn from watching the process used by the professor when engaged in problem-solving activities (Tuovinen and Sweller, 1999). *Demonstrations* are another type of modeling. A computer science professor might demonstrate how to use software to create a product, or a chemistry professor could demonstrate how to conduct a lab experiment before students have an opportunity to carry out the task independently. An instructor in a counseling course may demonstrate how to manage nonverbal communication when asking sensitive questions, and a graduate teaching assistant in chemistry may model structures of elements using Styrofoam balls and pipe cleaners. Research has shown that students who watched demonstrations learned more than students who did not (Balch, 2014). Although live demonstrations are typically best, research shows that virtual demonstrations are also effective (Lewis, 2015).

Applying newly acquired information can greatly facilitate learning. One of the most powerful ways we can increase student learning is through the application of concepts just learned. Learning cannot happen in isolation and without practice. The purpose of learning is to be able to use newly acquired skills and knowledge in a productive way. By providing real-world examples, we can help our students see how what they are learning can be transferred and used in a variety of situations. Showing students how the course content has meaning and relevance outside the classroom enhances student motivation and learning. Identifying real-world applications is therefore an essential part of the learning process. It provides a context for the new information being learned. Seeing the interrelatedness of concepts being learned and why they matter can have a positive, significant impact on the learning process.

CASE STUDIES

Real-life, complex, and in-depth case studies allow learners to use real-world examples to increase the meaning of our course content. McFarlane (2015) recommends choosing case studies that are relevant, practical, and interesting. In a study conducted by Mayo (2004), students were randomly assigned to case-based instruction classes or classes taught in the traditional lecture approach. Results indicated that most students found the case studies interesting and relevant, and students exposed to case studies performed significantly better on the final exam (85%) compared to students not exposed to case studies (75%). Case studies provide students with a context for taking in our course content. By increasing the content's meaning and application, we can deepen students' understanding while also increasing their motivation to learn the content. Although some view the case study approach as an alternative to the lecture, case studies can certainly be integrated into lectures. Professors can review a case study as part of the lecture or use the case study as an active learning break in between lecture segments. We can create our own case studies or use case studies that have already been developed by textbook authors or colleagues. In some instances with advanced students, the instructor can provide the anticipated learning outcome and ask students to create the cases, a process that can be a powerful learning experience.

It is important for the professor and the student to find real-world examples or applications of the content. Faculty should be providing initial examples for several reasons. As experts in the discipline and skilled educators, our examples will be on target and accurate. Sometimes, when students do not understand a concept, their examples may not correctly connect to the content. In addition, research has shown that students are better equipped to apply content after they have seen examples from the instructor. This was illustrated in a research study conducted by Carroll (1994) in which students were assigned to a worked example or practice group. In the worked example group, the teacher showed students how to do a variety of math problems. In the practice group, students instead worked independently on problems. The results indicated that students in the worked example group outperformed students in the practice group in class assignments, homework, and tests. These findings highlight the important role of expert examples.

Although instructor examples are important to learning, having students find examples as a way to reinforce a concept can also be a valuable exercise and provide an opportunity to engage students in a high-level cognitive task. This process strengthens elaboration, and research has shown that students learn more when they use elaborative techniques (Gadzella & Baloglu, 2003; Hall et al., 2004). Giving students the opportunity to engage in elaboration and find their own relevant examples during lectures is also a way to increase cognitive engagement. Because everyone's natural tendency is to look for meaning, students will often think of examples that illustrate the content to some extent during our lectures without even being prompted to do so. However, carving out lecture time for students to intentionally engage in this process will help them take full advantage of the benefits associated with this cognitive task. In addition to giving students the opportunity to cognitively interact with the content, asking students to identify examples also provides the instructor with an opportunity to assess the level of understanding among the students in the class. When students give their examples, we can then provide feedback to let students know if their examples are appropriate and accurate. This is an important part of the process because we don't want students to make inaccurate links or connections. Encouraging and assisting students with finding examples and real-world applications at different points of the lecture will also make it more likely they will apply this cognitive strategy outside the classroom. Wood, Motz, and Willoughby (1998) argue that students need more opportunities to practice using effective learning strategies. Students are most likely to use strategies that are familiar to them, so if we use this strategy regularly during our lectures, students will be more likely to incorporate the use of examples into their study approaches.

Lectures that include examples, models, cases, and demonstrations have been shown time and again to facilitate better learning in students. Providing case studies and other examples helps students think more critically about the course content. Because examples provide additional, meaningful information about the content, students will gain a more comprehensive understanding of the material. According to Bloom's taxonomy, application is an important cognitive task we typically tackle after developing a foundational knowledge and understanding of the new material (Anderson & Krathwohl, 2001). By applying what has been learned to different problems or situations, students can strengthen and deepen their understanding of the material. Application is an important and necessary part of learning, and we can assist students with developing sophisticated critical thinking skills by providing case studies and other examples and by having students engage in activities in which they must provide their own examples and consider how newly learned content can be applied to real-world situations.

LEARNING AND ENGAGEMENT STRATEGIES

Helping to make information meaningful through examples, such as modeling and demonstrations, has strong potential to augment lectures and increase elaboration for students. The following learning and engagement strategies are designed to illustrate a variety of ways to enhance traditional lectures through the use of examples. If you already use some of these lecture enhancement strategies, think of ways to adapt them for future use.

Provide Two Examples for Each Big Idea

Find a good example for each important concept in the course and then search for a complementary second example. If you have been teaching for a while, you probably already have examples you use regularly. If you are new to teaching or are teaching a new class, this task can seem overwhelming at first, but you do not have to do all this work yourself. Use your resources. Start by looking at the textbook you are using for the course. Most textbook authors provide numerous examples in the text as well as in the instructor resources that accompany the textbook. Of course, you can also search the Internet for examples. Many professional organizations have websites for faculty to share resources and ideas, which is another great place to start. Talking with colleagues in person or through electronic mailing lists or Google groups will also help you identify meaningful examples. Professional colleagues are often very willing to share the examples they use. A final strategy is to ask students to identify examples and then explain why they chose the specific example submitted. There are many places to find relevant examples for the major concepts in your course. Having at least two examples for each concept will be very helpful for your students.

Incorporate Case Studies

Case studies illustrate the real-world value of the concepts presented in your lectures. As mentioned earlier, case studies are more in-depth examples that highlight the relevance of the content learned through application. It is important to develop or find case studies that directly connect to your learning goals and to content specifically tied to presented lectures. Some case studies can simply be described, but it might be more effective to show videos of examples in other cases. For instance, in a marketing class, it might be best to show a video illustrating the business plan and actual advertisements used in a marketing project rather than trying to describe this process. Likewise, students will likely learn more from a video of an interview with someone who exhibits symptoms of a disorder rather than a verbal description of the symptoms. Just like with briefer examples, use resources from the publisher of your textbook, professional organizations, and colleagues on your campus to help you find case studies aligned with your learning goals. When presenting the case study, pause periodically so students can ask questions and reflect on what they are learning. It is also helpful to include the information gained through the case study in subsequent lectures.

Use Small-Group Discussions of Case Studies

Another way to use case studies is to have students discuss the scenario with other students in the class as a lecture check, rather than presenting the cases during the lecture. The small-group activity could take place after the content-based lecture. Small-group discussions of case studies often work best if you've already modeled how to analyze and approach the study and if you provide students with guiding questions or clear directions about the task. Students will then be able to refer to this previous experience and your modeling as they work on applying course content to the case study you provided. Depending on the complexity of the case study, this may take a considerable amount of class time, so you may want to ask students to do some of this work prior to attending class. When using this as an in-class activity, walk around the room to support and challenge students. A common but ineffective question often asked by professors when checking on the progress of a group is, "How is it going?" Students will often simply state all is well when you ask this question, and you are left without much information about their progress. Instead, ask more specific questions such as, "What is your response to this question?" or "What has surprised you about this case thus far?" These types of questions and subsequent responses allow you to better assess progress and provide useful feedback during this activity.

Be sure to give students adequate time in small groups to work through cases, but do not provide too much time. Keeping the time relatively short keeps students on task and uses class time efficiently. You can even turn the case into a small competition by handing out cases and stating, "When I say 'go' you will have only six minutes to complete the case. Let's see how many groups can finish in six minutes." As you experiment with using this technique, you will gain a better understanding of how much time is needed for the activity. Keep in mind that not providing students with enough time may frustrate students. Finding the right amount of time to help students stay on task and be productive is important. After groups have reported their case findings, provide a short lecture to summarize major points.

Create Make It Meaningful Teams

For this activity, assign students to teams or clusters of three to four individuals per group. Each Make it Meaningful team is tasked with coming up with an example of the concept you just discussed in your lecture. The goal is for students to work together to identify an example that is meaningful and relevant to them. In small classes, you can ask each group to share its example, but in larger classes, randomly select several groups to report on their examples. To keep others engaged during this part of the process, you could ask students to answer questions about the examples or have them rank the usefulness of the examples presented. Technology polling tools or online survey tools such as SurveyMonkey could be used for this purpose. Surveys could be incorporated into the activity during class or distributed electronically after class. On the survey, you could use simple questions such as, "Is this example on target and accurate?" and "How useful is this example in helping you to understand the content?" (A rating scale would work well for this question.) Adding this additional component to the process can help keep students on task during the small-group activity, and it can also provide you with valuable feedback about which examples resonated best with your students. You can then use these examples in future lectures.

Think, Pair, Share

This strategy is becoming ubiquitous in higher education and pairs extremely well with lectures. Examples are a great use of the think-pair-share activity, which asks students to first think independently of an example related to the content just presented in a lecture. After a minute or so (or longer with more complex content), students can then share their example with a classmate. You can then ask for volunteers or randomly call on several students to discuss some of the examples in a large group. During the large-group discussion, you can provide feedback about whether you believe the example is on target and add more details as needed.

Have Students Complete Example Tables

For this task, ask students to independently complete a two-column table. The first column is for the big ideas discussed during the lecture, and the second column is for the examples of the big ideas. As you have provided examples during the lecture, students should be able to easily find this information in their notes. After giving students a few minutes to complete the table, you can ask them to participate in a share-and-compare activity. Working with a partner, students share their examples, and if the examples are different, they can add the other examples to their table. This is a great activity for the end of class because it helps students summarize the examples and helps them see the important role of examples in learning, emphasizing that they should be looking for examples presented during lectures and documenting these examples in their notes.

Use a Web Quest

Ask students to search the Internet for an example of a concept being discussed. Students can work in pairs or small groups to do a quick search for an example of a concept just learned. You could also ask students to tweet their responses, and you could then display the examples on the screen for everyone to see. This is a great way to have students use technology during class for learning purposes. However, when you encourage students to use technology, you need to be mindful of the potential risk for off-task behaviors.

SUMMARY

Making lectures meaningful through examples promotes interest in the topics presented and allows students to use prior knowledge to better understand the new information being presented. Using relevant examples through modeling and demonstration allows for students to make sense of what they are learning and also provides elaboration to aid in remembering the material when it is needed at a later time. Meaning is essential for elaboration of the information being learned, and examples are important to facilitate that meaning, which in turn fosters long-term learning.

REFERENCES

Anderson, L. W., & Krathwohl, D. R. (2001). *A taxonomy for learning, teaching, and assessing: A revision of Bloom's taxonomy of educational objectives*. New York, NY: Longman.

Balch, W. R. (2014). A referential communication demonstration versus a lecture-only control: Learning benefits. *Teaching of Psychology, 41*(3), 213–219.

Baldwin, J. M. (1889). *Handbook of psychology*. New York, NY: Henry Holt.

Bandura, A., & Walters, R. H. (1963). *Social learning and personality development*. New York, NY: Holt, Rinehart & Winston.

Carroll, W. M. (1994). Using worked examples as an instructional support in the algebra classroom. *Journal of Educational Psychology, 86*, 360–367. doi:10.1037/0022-0663.86.3.360

Gadzella, B., & Baloglu, M. (2003). High and low achieving education students on processing, retaining, and retrieval of information. *Journal of Instructional Psychology, 30*, 99–103.

Goodman, S., Jaffer, T., Keresztesi, M., Mamdani, F., Mokgatle, D., Musariri, M., & . . . Schlechter, A. (2011). An investigation of the relationship between students' motivation and academic performance as mediated by effort. *South African Journal of Psychology, 41*, 373–385. doi:10.1177/008124631104100311

Hall, N., Hladkyi, S., Perry, R., & Ruthig, J. (2004). The role of attributional retraining and elaborative learning in college students' academic development. *Journal of Social Psychology, 144*, 591–612.

Hamilton, R. J. (1997). Effects of three types of elaboration on learning concepts from text. *Contemporary Educational Psychology, 22*, 299–318. doi:10.1006/ceps.1997.0935

Lewis, J. L. (2015). A comparison between two different activities for teaching learning principles: Virtual animal labs versus human demonstrations. *Scholarship of Teaching and Learning in Psychology, 1*, 182–188. doi:10.1037/stl0000013

Mayo, J. A. (2004). Using case-based instruction to bridge the gap between theory and practice in psychology of adjustment. *Journal of Constructivist Psychology, 17*, 137–146. doi:10.1080/10720530490273917

McFarlane, D. A. (2015). Guidelines for using case studies in the teaching-learning process. *College Quarterly, 18*(1),1–6.

Piaget, J. (2001). *The psychology of intelligence*. New York: NY: Routledge Classics.

Rogers, T. B., Kuiper, N. A., & Kirker, W. S. (1977). Self-reference and the encoding of personal information. *Journal of Personality and Social Psychology, 35*: 677–678. doi:10.1037/0022-3514.35.9.677

Tuovinen, J. E., & Sweller, J. (1999). A comparison of cognitive load associated with discovery learning and worked examples. *Journal of Educational Psychology, 91*, 334–341. doi:10.1037/0022-0663.91.2.334

Walker, C. O., Greene, B. A., & Mansell, R. A. (2006). Identification with academics, intrinsic/extrinsic motivation, and self-efficacy as predictors of cognitive engagement. *Learning and Individual Differences, 16*(1), 1–12. doi:10.1016/j.lindif.2005.06.004

Waschull, S. B. (2005). Predicting success in online psychology courses: Self-discipline and motivation. *Teaching of Psychology, 32*, 190–192. doi:10.1207/s15328023top3203_11

Wlodkowski, R. J., & Ginsberg, M. B., (1995). *Diversity and motivation: Culturally responsive teaching in college*. New York, NY: Jossey-Bass.

Wood, E., Motz, M., & Willoughby, T. (1998). Examining students' retrospective memories of strategy development. *Journal of Educational Psychology, 90*, 698–704. doi:10.1037/0022-0663.90.4.698

Wood, E., Willoughby, T., McDermott, C., Motz, M., Kaspar, V., & Ducharme, M. J. (1999). Developmental differences in study behavior. *Journal of Educational Psychology, 91*, 527–536. doi:10.1037/0022-0663.91.3.527

7

REFLECTION OPPORTUNITIES

"Reflecting simply put is the act of thinking about something while seeking a deeper level of understanding" (Bard, 2014, p. 1). Reflection increases cognitive engagement, which is important because cognitive engagement plays a major role in learning (Mayer, 2009). Research demonstrates that learning increases when reflection activities take place (Conrad, 2013), and reflection activities can facilitate the development of critical thinking skills (Colley, Bilics, & Lerch, 2012). Because faculty understand the important role reflection has in the learning process, there has been an increase in the use of reflection-based assignments in recent years. An example of a reflection-based assignment is the exam wrapper, which requires students to reflect on whether the learning strategies they used led to desired outcomes on an exam and then to develop an action plan for the next exam (Ambrose et al., 2010). Reflective journals are also often used by faculty, especially in disciplines such as education and nursing, to help students continually monitor their learning progress and make adjustments as needed to improve their performance on various tasks.

Reflection assignments help students achieve course learning goals and can also be done during class. In fact, one of the most powerful ways we can improve how we lecture is to build in time for reflection during the class period. Some may argue that reflection is best left as an exercise for outside of class because the limited amount of class time is needed for delivering content. However, it is important to recognize that covering more information does not always lead to higher levels of learning. In fact, it is more likely that learning will be reduced when learners experience information overload (Burrows, 2002; Kaczmarzyk et al., 2013). There is only so much information an individual can take in without having an opportunity to process the content in some way, which is one of the reasons the lecture has developed such a bad reputation. Some lecturers talk at students for an entire class period without giving them a chance to process and reflect on the information being learned. As a result, students get to a point in the class period where they are simply not able to process more information and become mentally exhausted.

By breaking up lectures into smaller, more manageable chunks and giving students in-class time to process each chunk of information before moving on, student learning can be increased. Researchers have also found that giving students an opportunity to engage in reflection immediately after learning works better than delaying the reflection activity (Embo, Driessen, Valcke, & Van Der Vleuten, 2014). Another important reason to use class time for this activity is that it communicates that faculty highly value reflection. How we spend our class time sends powerful messages to our students about what is and is not important. Including time for reflection in class will communicate to our students that reflection plays an important part in learning and is therefore a worthwhile activity.

What is reflection, and how can it be used in our classes? *Reflection* is a broad term that has several meanings and applications to learning. Contextual reflection involves understanding the new content in the context of our current knowledge (Smith, 2011). Although new information may be able to be assimilated into existing structures, in some cases our current knowledge structures will need to be modified to accommodate the new information, and in still other cases new organizational schemas will need to be created during this process. Muncy (2014) emphasized that one of the primary tasks of reflection is to understand content more deeply by discovering connections between the new material and prior knowledge. Reflective activities that are contextual in nature facilitate the understanding of new content by helping students activate relevant, prior knowledge and identify meaningful connections among concepts.

Another type of reflection is personal reflection (Smith, 2011), which plays an important role in self-regulatory processes. It is important for students to become skilled at self-regulatory behaviors, as positive outcomes are associated with these skills. Students who are effective self-regulators are more likely to persist on tasks (Chen, 2011). When we ask students to engage in personal reflection about their learning, it is critical to draw their attention to factors that are within their control. In other words, we can help students see that their success or failure is because of, at least in part, internal, changeable factors such as effort. Research has consistently shown that this type of thinking leads to the best outcomes (Dweck, 2006). Engaging in personal reflection not only helps students better monitor progress toward goals and determine when adjustments are needed to stay on track with their goals but also helps facilitate a productive mind-set that will lead to high levels of perseverance and ultimately goal achievement. This is particularly true when personal reflection activities require students to reflect on their learning behaviors and experiences and to identify action plans that will lead to positive outcomes. Research has shown that mind-set–based interventions have been particularly helpful to students from underrepresented groups (Aronson, Fried, & Good, 2002). Thus, although these interventions can be of value to all students, cognitive interventions aimed at helping students focus primarily on internal factors related to successes and failures may be even more helpful to some student populations.

We can use reflection along with lectures in several different ways. From a contextual or content perspective, reflection can be an opportunity for students to digest new content, make connections between new and previously learned concepts, or to think more deeply about the content by identifying examples of the concepts just learned. Giving students an opportunity to reflect on content just learned during class will help students develop a stronger understanding of content being learned. Reflection can also focus on process as opposed to content. Having students reflect on how well they are learning the content and how their actions prior to and during class have influenced their learning can facilitate self-regulation skills. The Muddiest Point version of the one-minute papers is an example of how reflection can be used for this purpose as it asks students to think about which concepts they are having difficulty understanding. This type of reflection prompts the student to take action such as rereading the related section of the text, working with a classmate, or contacting the professor. This is, of course, the purpose of the self-regulation process, to make changes as needed so that goals can be achieved.

Research strongly supports using reflective activities during class, providing us with evidence that pausing our lecture to give students the opportunity to process and reflect on the information just learned is a valuable use of class time. Students learn more when given time to reflect and cognitively engage with the content. Ruhl, Hughes, and Schloss (1987) conducted a research study of students either in a pause or no-pause learning group. The course sections, not the students, were randomly designated pause or no pause. Students in the pause classes were given three 2-minute pauses during a 45-minute lecture. During each pause, students were asked to review their notes and discuss them with a classmate. The professor determined when the break fit best during the lecture. The range of time spent lecturing in between breaks was 12 to 18 minutes. Students in the pause classes, where 6 minutes of lecture time was used instead for students to process the lecture content with a classmate, outperformed students in the no-pause classes on immediate recall of concepts and also on an objective test taken 12 days later. More specifically, students in the pause classes remembered on average 22.97 concepts, whereas students in the no-pause classes only recalled an average of 16.63 concepts. The average score on the objective test, administered 12 days after the lecture, was 84.39 for students in the pause classes and 76.28 for students in the no-pause condition classes (Ruhl et al., 1987). These findings are not only statistically significant but also demonstrate a practical level of significance. Students in the pause group scored nearly a full letter grade higher on the test.

The power of pausing was also demonstrated in a study with first-year medical students (Bachhel & Thaman, 2014). Students in the experimental group were given 2 to 3 minutes after every 12 to 15 minutes of lecture to work with a partner to compare notes. The control group attended a lecture without a pause. On a multiple-choice test that was given 15 days after the lecture, students who were in the experimental pause group performed significantly better on a 30-question multiple-choice test compared to the control group.

The tasks students engage in during a lecture pause do matter. Some tasks lead to higher recall and performance than others. Davis and Hult (1997) randomly assigned students to one of three conditions: written summary pause, reviewing notes pause, or no pause. All students watched the same 21-minute videotaped lecture. The written summary and reviewing notes groups were given two 4-minute pauses to perform their required activity. On a free recall task, students in the pause groups performed better than students in the no pause group, but the written summary group recalled the highest number of concepts (10.92) compared to the reviewing notes (8.04) and no pause (6.87) groups (Davis & Hult, 1997). Writing a summary of what has been learned during a lecture is one of the best ways for students to process information. In another study involving nearly 1,000 undergraduates, Drabick, Weisberg, Paul, and Bubier (2007) also found that writing during a pause from a lecture led to the best outcome. Specifically, pausing to write rather than to think was associated with better performance on multiple-choice questions that assessed factual and conceptual knowledge (Drabick et al., 2007).

Reflection opportunities need not take up much class time at all. Spending even one minute during a class on reflection can have positive results. The one-minute paper is an example of how literally just one minute of class time can enhance learning. Researchers have found assigning students a one-minute paper at the end of a statistics class to summarize what they learned to be positively connected to higher levels of learning (Das, 2010). Almer, Jones, and Moeckel (1998) studied the impact of the one-minute papers on quiz grades. They also investigated the impact of grading the one-minute papers and students' ability levels. Twenty different sections of the course were randomly assigned to a variety of conditions. Students who completed a one-minute paper scored almost an entire letter grade higher on an essay quiz than students who did not complete a one-minute paper. Interestingly, students performed better on the quiz when the one-minute paper was not graded. Almer and colleagues (1998) suggested this might be because of an artifact of the study, namely that students had access to nongraded one-minute papers. The graded papers were not available to students because the professor retained them for grading. Another important finding was that there was no difference between high- and low-ability students, indicating that all students benefitted from participating in the one-minute paper exercise (Almer et al., 1998).

The nature of the reflective prompt can also play an important role in how much the reflection activity can improve learning. Lee and Hutchison (1998), for example, found that more challenging reflective questions led to higher learning. In particular, questions asking "why" were connected to the highest levels of learning. This is consistent with learning theory as tasks that are more challenging require deeper processing, which in turn leads to higher levels of achievement. As you help your students build their foundational knowledge in your discipline, the reflection prompts may change. For instance, in the beginning of the semester, prompts may focus on learning key vocabulary and identifying examples. As students' foundational knowledge increases, the difficulty level of your question prompts can also increase. In other words, the tasks can become more cognitively complex as the semester progresses.

Lee and Hutchison (1998) also found the quality of the student response makes a difference in terms of how much the reflection activity positively affects learning. It is therefore not just a pause that matters but how much cognitive effort the students are putting forth during the pause. The accuracy and depth of their responses will undoubtedly have an impact on the usefulness of the exercise. Fortunately, Muncy (2014) found that 99% of journal entries reviewed in a study provided evidence that students put effort into reflection, with 51% showing extensive levels of reflection. Although these data provide some evidence that students do in fact put forth effort on reflection tasks, it is still important to review reflection work at least periodically. This is particularly important when using contextual reflection that requires students to process the content to confirm the accuracy of their understanding. Providing feedback on every reflection activity may not be feasible or even desirable, although it is important to take advantage of this formative assessment feedback opportunity whenever possible. By reviewing student responses on contextual reflection activities, we can find out whether students understand our lectures and if they are able to differentiate the important content from the less important material. This can guide our teaching practices. For example, if students are not fully understanding a concept, we can provide different or additional examples or explanations to help increase their understanding before moving on to additional content. Providing at least overall feedback, even if it is directed at the group rather than individuals, can help students know whether their responses are on target.

How often should we use reflection exercises during class? As discussed in Chapter 4, there is not much research to guide us in this area. Prince (2004) recommends that we give students an opportunity to reflect on content after about 15 minutes of lecture, at which point students may be in information overload and attention is more likely to wander. However, it is important for us to remember that we need to consider many variables other than how much time has passed when determining when to use a reflection pause. Some other important variables to consider are the complexity of the content, the background knowledge of the students, the relevance and meaning of the content, the interest level of the student, and attention. A cognitively engaging activity can give students time to process information just learned before needing to take in additional new content.

Muncy (2014) offers four factors to consider when asking students to complete reflection assignments.

1. Determine the purpose of the reflection. Sharing the rationale behind the activity can increase the likelihood that students will put forth significant effort during the task and helps keep us focused on the course learning goals.
2. Consider how often students should engage in reflective activities in and outside the classroom and our expectations in terms of length, content, and quality.
3. Establish and explain grading criteria if reflections are to be read and graded.
4. Determine if you will you use online tools such as blogs. If so, consider whether they will be private or open to the class.

Reflection is not just a valuable activity for college students. Successful professionals regularly engage in contextual and personal reflection to improve performance and achieve high-level goals. Thus, teaching this skill will not only help students meet with success in college but also serve them well later in life. The "Personal Reflective Learning Log" (2015) that was published in the *British Journal of School Nursing* is a professional example of contextual reflection. In this example, nurses who just read an article on adolescent sexual behavior were asked to answer content questions, summarize what was learned, and apply this content to a case scenario. Many of us also regularly engage in personal reflection, thinking about what went well and what might not have gone as well when teaching. As we just discussed, we can even read student responses to reflective exercises as one form of feedback. Bard (2014) encourages educators to formally engage in the process of reflection to improve our teaching practices. Thus, reflection is a skill that is needed in college and beyond. By demonstrating the value of this exercise to our students now, we can help build and foster this skill that will serve them well now and in the future.

LEARNING AND ENGAGEMENT STRATEGIES

Reflection is an important component to integrating new information into existing information. With respect to lectures, reflection can be a particularly valuable activity to confirm understanding and to promote transfer of knowledge. Reflection can also assist students with becoming better self-regulators, which can positively affect learning. The following learning and engagement strategies are designed to provide examples of a variety of ways to enhance traditional lectures through reflection. It you already use some of these lecture enhancement strategies, think of ways to adapt them for future use.

One-Minute Papers

These assignments can be literally just one-minute breaks in which students are asked to write a response to a question posed by the professor following a lecture segment (Angelo & Cross, 1993). It should be noted that it is not a requirement that the writing be only one minute. It can be two or three minutes. The most important consideration is that it is a brief pause. The responses may be recorded in a notebook or journal for students' personal use only or may be written on an index card or piece of paper that is turned in to the professor. It can be graded or ungraded. There are many different ways a one-minute paper can be used to give students an opportunity to reflect during a lecture or class lesson. The following are the most common questions: "What are the most important concepts from today's lecture?" and "What concepts from today are not clear to you?"

The second question is often referred to as *the muddiest point.* This combination of questions prompts students to engage in content- and process-based reflection. The first question asks students to focus on the content or most important points, whereas the second question focuses on the learning process, asking students to make a judgment about which concepts were not clear. There are, however, many different variations of the one-minute paper. Think about what types of questions would work best in your discipline. The following are some sample prompts for a one-minute paper:

- What is an example of this concept?
- How does this concept relate to a previously learned concept?
- What is the most interesting fact or skill you learned today?
- A classmate contacts you because he or she was unable to attend class today. What were the big ideas from today's lecture that you would share with your classmate?

Index Card Fast Pass Conversation Exercise

An index card passing exercise works well in the beginning of class to give students an opportunity to reflect on what was learned during a previous lecture or from the readings, as a midclass opportunity to summarize concepts discussed thus far in lecture, or as a great way to review concepts from an entire lecture at the end of class. Students are asked to write their response to a prompt, such as, "What was the most important concept discussed today?" on an index card and told that they do not need to put their name on the index card. Students are informed that they will soon exchange cards with other students. Informing students that their card will be read by others encourages them to clearly communicate ideas. Once students are finished responding to a provided prompt, ask them to stand up, move around the room, and exchange cards until you say stop or use some other signal. When they are exchanging cards, they do not read or discuss the cards until they are directed to do so. At that point, students should find a student or two who is within physical proximity, and then they discuss the content of the cards. Students can stand up for this activity as they will typically only discuss the content for a few minutes before finding a new partner. After a few minutes, signal for the conversations to stop and tell students to repeat the process, exchanging cards with classmates again. Once again, you'll signal students to stop and talk with a classmate or two who is standing nearby. Students will review and discuss the concepts on the index cards they are currently holding. If time permits, you can repeat the steps once more, or you can stop the activity after two rounds. An advantage of this reflection exercise is that it combines cognitive and social engagement strategies. From a social standpoint, students are likely interacting with classmates with whom they may not typically talk during class. This is a great way to foster connections and promote higher level critical thinking skills because students will have the chance to hear about the topic from different perspectives. In addition, the index card fast pass conversation activity gives students an opportunity to move around for a few minutes, which can help them be more focused once they return to the lecture portion of class. Research has shown that physical activity energizes learners and leads to enhanced academic performance (Erwin, Fedewa, & Ahn, 2012). Physical movement can be particularly advantageous in longer classes.

News Report

This activity involves two students working together to determine the three most important concepts of that day's lecture. Encourage students to think of themselves as news anchors who have only a minute or two to communicate the most important points about a news story. Once they identify the three main points, each group of partners should decide who will be the news reporter and who will be the videographer. They should take turns each time this activity takes place so everyone gets to be the reporter. Give students a few minutes to videotape the informal newscast using the cameras on their phones. Students can then share these news reports electronically, or you can ask for student volunteers to show their videos to the class. The videotaped newscasts can later be used during an exam review session or by students as a study tool. Another option is to forego the videotaping and ask some students to come to the front of the room to give a live newscast. Whether you use the live or video approach, this is an excellent way to help focus students on the big ideas of the lecture. You may want to check for accuracy before students begin the video or live newscast. You can combine the news report with the one-minute paper by having students share their muddiest points and then ask students to choose one of the muddiest points listed by a classmate as the subject matter for the newscast. In other words, each group of partners should choose one of the muddiest points they believe they understand well and create a newscast. If everyone in the class is confused by a concept, then you might want to step in and do the newscast yourself.

This approach allows peer-to-peer teaching on elements students need assistance with learning.

Concept Map Comparisons

Concept maps are excellent visual tools that clearly show hierarchies and connections among concepts learned in lecture. For this activity, students can work alone or in a small group to create a map of the important concepts discussed during the lecture. If you are communicating three main points during a discussion lecture, you may want to pause after each point and ask students to generate a concept map or add to the one they just started rather than waiting until the end of class. The visual nature of the connections between concepts can be a powerful learning tool. A variation of this activity is to have students create a table or matrix. You may provide students with a partially completed concept map or table or give students a blank form. The concept maps or tables they create can be used as study tools. As students become more comfortable with these note-taking approaches, it is more likely they will use these approaches outside class. This is very valuable because the act of organizing lecture content has been associated with positive academic outcomes (Kiewra, DuBois, Christian, & McShane, 1988).

Think, Pair, Share

This is one of the most commonly used reflection activities and pairs well with any lecture format (Lyman, 1981). The first part of the process is for students to independently reflect on the content by thinking about their answer to the question or prompt. Some faculty will encourage students to write down their thoughts during this part of the process. Second, students find, or may be assigned, a partner. For the sake of convenience and to save class time, faculty will often have students work with a classmate sitting nearby. It is advantageous for students to have an opportunity to work with different students, but the benefit of this approach needs to be weighed against the cost of the time needed for students to find different partners. During this second step of the process, students should discuss their responses and ideas with their partner. The third step involves a large-group discussion. All students do not need to contribute to the large-group conversation. Rather, you will likely want to hear from a few students. This is an excellent time to randomly call on students because they have had time to process and discuss the issue, and this will give you an opportunity to hear students who may not typically volunteer to participate in class discussions. It is important for you to tell students up front that you will be randomly selecting them to share their ideas with the class. The advantage of this approach instead of a large-group discussion is that every student in the class is involved and participating in some way even if it's not at the whole-class level. Given the diverse student body in most college classrooms, this also gives students an opportunity to interact with students from different backgrounds and with different perspectives, adding to the learning experience. Because some faculty find the small-group activity a much better option than large-group discussions, they may replace the *share* with *square*. To do this, instead of a whole-class discussion after the pair portion, the faculty member has each pair find one other pair to discuss further. *Square* simply refers to the shape of the group when four students are talking. You may also want to use this approach if many of your students are from cultures where speaking in public is not the norm, and this smaller conversation may be better suited to your student population.

Review and Compare Notes

This strategy provides students with an opportunity to pause and process key information just learned during the lecture with a classmate. A benefit of this approach is that students get the chance to work with one another to see if they agree about which content was most important. Students can also use this time to fill in any information gaps if needed. This is particularly helpful if a student's mind was wandering for a few minutes of the lecture. As the professor, you may want to provide students with some structure for this activity. For example, you could tell them to circle, underline, or highlight content they both captured in their notes. You could also ask them to discuss why they did or did not write down concepts, an activity that combines contextual and personal reflection. This activity can also work well at the start of class, asking students to compare notes from the reading assignment.

Reflective Journal

This activity is designed to help students engage in personal reflection. The reflective journal is a tool for the student to think about how well he or she is learning the lecture content and identify ways to increase learning as needed. The following are some examples of questions students can respond to during or at the end of class:

- What is my level of understanding of the content presented so far or today?

- What actions did I engage in prior to class that are helping me learn this content?
- What actions am I engaging in during class to help me learn the content?
- What actions can I take after class to increase my understanding of this content?

If you use the reflective journal at various times throughout the semester, the compilation of journals becomes a record of students' learning behaviors and progress. This can serve as a foundation for a larger, more in-depth reflection activity such as a midsemester or an end-of-semester reflection assignment. As with all reflection activities, the reflection journal may be graded or ungraded. Some faculty may not collect or grade the journals during the semester but instead grade a reflection assignment that is based on the reflection journal. Other faculty may view this as a personal journal that should not be read by others and would therefore not grade it. One significant advantage of the reflective journal is that it can facilitate a growth mind-set by focusing student attention on internal, changeable attributes. This happens through carefully crafted question prompts that direct attention toward controllable factors. When students attribute their successes and failures to factors, such as effort, that are within their control, they are more likely to meet with success in the future (Dweck, 2006). In fact, having a positive, productive mind-set is one of the most important characteristics of successful people.

Tweet Summaries

Twitter or other similar social media tools can be used for reflective purposes during class lectures or between mini lectures. Tweet summaries involve asking students to identify a main idea, another concept that might be related to the topic being discussed, an example, or even confusing concepts. The limited number of characters allowed in a tweet requires students to think about what is most important. The Twitter feed can then be projected onto a screen so that everyone can see it during class. You and your students will also be able to access it after class. One of the advantages of this approach is that you can quickly scan the responses to determine the extent to which students understand the lecture content. It also gives you an opportunity to immediately address inaccuracies and highlight or emphasize target responses such as excellent examples. Another advantage is that the class responses are accessible later and can be used as a study tool. Some possible disadvantages, however, are students may not have

Twitter accounts or do not wish to use their accounts for this purpose, and it is possible for inappropriate or inaccurate content to be posted to the Twitter feed. In addition, after the social media reflection is finished, you'll need to have a strategy to get students to return their focus to the lecture and course content.

Blogs and Wikis

Blogs and wikis, online tools for sharing information, are also effective ways to use technology to reflect on material learned in lecture. Blogs typically have only one primary author, so they can look very similar to the reflective journal, except they are online. The chronological sequence makes it easy to track progress over time. Wikis, in contrast, tend to have multiple contributors and might be a good tool for promoting contextual reflection. For example, you could ask the class to cocreate a study guide as a wiki. Blogging can also be used for this purpose, but blogging may be the better option for personal reflection exercises (if private settings are used). Although many faculty who use blogging as an assignment ask students to complete the blogs outside class, blogging can also be done during class. If students have mobile devices and Internet access, the blog content can be immediately put into the online reflective journal. If technology limitations prohibit this from happening immediately, students can write their blogs during class and then post them later in the day when they have the technology access they need. One of the advantages of blogging versus using a paper reflective journal is that we can more easily monitor whether students are completing the task effectively and can provide feedback, if desired, without having to spend class time on collecting and returning the reflections. In addition, the online format provides a useful organizational structure that can serve as a study tool and be a way for students to see how they have grown as learners. Finally, blog and wiki material is often exceptional content to include in future lectures with a note that the material was developed by students.

SUMMARY

Reflection is an integral part of the learning process when used in conjunction with the lecture. Reflection helps the student bring her or his own voice into the process and also allows elaboration of the content. The strategies presented in this chapter assist in giving a framework by which the student can digest the course content and monitor learning progress.

REFERENCES

Almer, E. D., Jones, K., & Moeckel, C. L. (1998). The impact of one-minute papers on learning in an introductory accounting course. *Issues in Accounting Education, 13*, 485–497.

Ambrose, S. A., Bridges, M. W., DiPietro, M., Lovett, M. C., & Norman, M. K. (2010). *How learning works: 7 research-based principles for smart teaching.* San Francisco, CA: Jossey-Bass.

Angelo, T. A., & Cross, K. P. (1993). *Classroom assessment techniques: A handbook for college teachers.* San Francisco, CA: Jossey-Bass.

Aronson, J., Fried, C. B., & Good, C. (2002). Reducing the effects of stereotype threat on African American college students by shaping theories of intelligence. *Journal of Experimental Social Psychology, 38*, 113–126.

Bachhel, R., & Thaman, R. G. (2014). Effective use of pause procedure to enhance student engagement and learning. *Journal of Clinical & Diagnostic Research, 8*(8), 1–3. doi:10.7860/JCDR/2014/8260.4691

Bard, R. (2014). Focus on learning: Reflective learners & feedback. *TESL-EJ, 18*(3), 1–18.

Burrows, D. (2002). Memory overload: The effects of amount of information, rate of presentation, and reorganization. *Cognitive Technology, 7*(1), 20–30.

Chen, P. (2011). Guiding college students to develop academic self-regulatory skills. *Journal of College Teaching & Learning, 8*(9), 29–34.

Colley, B. M., Bilics, A. R., & Lerch, C. M. (2012). Reflection: A key component to thinking critically. *Canadian Journal for the Scholarship of Teaching and Learning, 3*(1), 1–19.

Conrad, N. J. (2013). Practicing what is preached: Self-reflections on memory in a memory course. *Teaching of Psychology, 40*, 44–47. doi:10.1177/0098628312465863

Das, A. (2010). Econometric assessment of "One Minute" paper as a pedagogic tool. *International Education Studies, 3*(1), 17–22.

Davis, M., & Hult, R. E. (1997). Effects of writing summaries as a generative learning activity during note taking. *Teaching of Psychology, 24*, 47–50.

Drabick, D. A. G., Weisberg, R., Paul, L., & Bubier, J. L. (2007). Methods and techniques: Keeping it short and sweet: Brief, ungraded writing assignments facilitate learning. *Teaching of Psychology, 34*, 172–176.

Dweck, C. S. (2006). *Mindset: The new psychology of success.* New York, NY: Random House.

Embo, M. C., Driessen, E., Valcke, M., & Van Der Vleuten, C. M. (2014). Scaffolding reflective learning in clinical practice: A comparison of two types of reflective activities. *Medical Teacher, 36*, 602–607. doi:10.3109/0142159X.2014.899686

Erwin, H., Fedewa, A., & Ahn, S. (2012). Student academic performance outcomes of a classroom physical activity intervention: A pilot study. *International Electronic Journal of Elementary Education, 4*, 473–487.

Kaczmarzyk, M., Francikowski, J., Łozowski, B., Rozpędek, M., Sawczyn, T., & Sułowicz, S. (2013). The bit value of working memory. *Psychology & Neuroscience, 6*, 345–349. doi:10.3922/j.psns.2013.3.11

Kiewra, K., DuBois, N., Christian, D., & McShane, A. (1988). Providing study notes: Comparison of three types of notes for review. *Journal of Educational Psychology, 80*, 595–597. doi:10.1037/0022-0663.80.4.595

Lee, A. Y., & Hutchison, L. (1998). Improving learning from examples through reflection. *Journal of Experimental Psychology: Applied, 4*, 187–210. doi:10.1037/1076-898X.4.3.187

Lyman, F. T. (1981). The responsive classroom discussion: The inclusion of all students. In A. Anderson (Ed.), *Mainstreaming digest* (pp. 109–113). College Park: University of Maryland Press.

Mayer, R. E. (2009) *Multimedia learning* (2nd ed.). New York, NY: Cambridge University Press.

Muncy, J. A. (2014). Blogging for reflection: The use of online journals to engage students in reflective learning. *Marketing Education Review, 24*, 101–113.

Personal reflective learning log. (2015). *British Journal of School Nursing, 9*, 363–364.

Prince, M. (2004). Does active learning work? A review of the research. *Journal of Engineering Education. 93*, 223–231.

Ruhl, K. L., Hughes, C. A., & Schloss, P. J. (1987). Using the pause procedure to enhance lecture recall. *Teacher Education and Special Education, 10*(1), 14–18.

Smith, E. (2011). Teaching critical reflection. *Teaching in Higher Education, 16*, 211–223.

8

RETRIEVAL PRACTICE

As presented in Chapter 3, there are three phases of the learning and memory process: encoding, storage, and retrieval (Atkinson & Shiffrin, 1968; Myers, 2014). When thinking about how to help our students learn course content, the focus is almost exclusively on the first two phases, encoding and storage. Attending lectures, taking notes, and reading in preparation for class are all processes pertaining to encoding and storage and associated with learning. Retrieval, however, is considered to be simply the act of accessing information from our memory system that has been encoded (learned) and stored (memorized). In many respects, individuals consider retrieval to be the test as to whether something has been learned or not. However, recent research on the retrieval process has demonstrated that retrieval plays an important role in the process of learning and remembering (Roediger & Karpicke, 2006a).

"Repeated recall appears to help memory consolidate into a cohesive representation in the brain and to strengthen and multiply the neural routes by which the knowledge can be retrieved" (Brown, Roediger, & McDaniel, 2014, p. 28). In other words, the more you retrieve the content, the more efficiently you will access that content in the future. As a result of repeatedly retrieving this information, your memory for the content is strengthened. Neuroscientists have described this process as "long-term potentiation," and documented the tremendous benefit of this process (Doyle & Zakrajsek, 2013, pp. 6–7). An analogy that often helps students understand the importance of retrieval is the pattern of paths in the grass that appear on nearly every campus. If you are the first person to take a shortcut as you walk from one building to another building and there are no walkways, you will likely leave foot impressions in the grass that will disappear within a short period of time. As you (and your classmates) use this same shortcut over and over again, you will notice that a pathway starts to form. At first the grass is pressed down, then the grass is sparse, and after a period of time a dirt path will develop and continue to be packed down. After much use grass will not grow in the path at all as the dirt has become very compacted. Once the compacted dirt path has been established, it will persist for a long time, even if everyone stops taking that shortcut. When you look at a well-established path, it is obvious where the path leads. The more worn the path, the more obvious the place it leads to, and the longer it will remain when used infrequently. A similar process works with learning and memory. The more you retrieve and use material previously encoded and stored, the stronger the neural path and the easier it will be for you to find the information when needed. Once the neuron path is worn enough, you may be able to recall the information decades later, even if it is not regularly retrieved.

The opposite process happens for information that is not retrieved often enough to make a groove in a neuron pathway. This is the foundation for the phrase "use it or lose it." Information that is not retrieved and used is often forgotten. This is very beneficial for humans as most of the information we process should be forgotten, and the brain uses this process to remove unneeded information. Our brains make the assumption that if information is not retrieved and used several times after receiving it, it is simply not necessary for the information to occupy valuable storage space for later retrieval. Examples of this kind of information include the color of the car driving in the lane next to you on the way to campus, what you had for lunch last Tuesday, and the name of a store you walked past this morning. Unfortunately, the process is the same for academic content. If information is not retrieved and used in some way it fades quickly from memory systems and will not be easily available for retrieval when desired.

In academic situations, retrieval is the primary method to determine whether something has been learned and now resides in one's memory. Calling on students in class is one way to test memory by asking a student to retrieve desired information. In the academy, grades are primarily based on how much a student knows or can think about a given topic. The most efficient and consistent mechanism to determine the extent of information in long-term memory is testing, one of the most widely used mechanisms or tools for retrieval purposes. Testing allows us to get a sense of what exists in the memory system, discovering how much a student has learned. In other words, testing is typically thought of as a way to measure academic achievement. Historically, many professors gave only two major tests: a midterm and a final exam. However, this practice is changing because recent research has emphasized that testing is a way not only to demonstrate knowledge to assign a grade but also to learn information in a way that makes it available at a later date. That is, we now know that testing is a powerful memory tool. Taking a test helps you remember and learn the content more effectively because it requires you to retrieve the information. If you are tested often, the material forms grooves similar to the shortcut described earlier. This phenomenon has been called the *testing effect* (Einstein, 2012; Roediger & Karpicke, 2006b).

Roediger and Karpicke (2006b) studied the testing effect by randomly assigning research participants to one of the following conditions:

- study, study, study, study (SSSS)
- study, study, study, test (SSST)
- study, test, test, test (STTT)

In each study part, students were given 5 minutes to learn the content in a passage. Students in SSSS therefore had 20 minutes to learn the content, whereas students in SSST had 15 minutes, and the students in STTT had just 5 minutes to learn the content. In the test part, students were asked to recall as much as they could remember about the passage and write down what they remembered. The students in SSSS were not given an opportunity to participate in this recall task. The students in SSST had a single 5-minute opportunity to engage in free recall after having 15 minutes to learn the content. The STTT students only had access to the passage for 5 minutes and spent the remainder of the time (15 minutes) recalling the passage multiple times. All students were given a test on the content 5 minutes after the activity was complete and then again a week later (Roediger & Karpicke, 2006b).

Results indicated that students who engaged in study multiple times with no test practice performed the best on the test that was given five minutes after the completion of the activity. Specifically, the amount of content recalled five minutes after the activity was 83% for the SSSS group, 78% for the SSST group, and 71% for the STTT group. However, when the test was given again one week later, the results had completely reversed. On this delayed recall test, students in the STTT group performed significantly better than the other two groups, remembering 61% of the content compared to the SSST group that recalled 56% and the SSSS group that only recalled 40% of the content (Roediger & Karpicke, 2006b). Note the magnitude of these differences. The group that read the information one time and practiced retrieving the information three times recalled 50% more information than those who studied the information multiple times without practicing recall. Thus, this study highlights the important role testing plays in the long-term retention of material being learned. It is important to note that this is not an isolated finding. Rather, the powerful role of testing in learning has been consistently demonstrated in numerous studies (Karpicke & Roediger, 2007; Logan, Thompson, & Marshak, 2011; Meyer & Logan, 2013; Roediger, Agarwal, McDaniel, & McDermott, 2011).

Although the research on the power of testing is very clear, students still often underestimate the importance of incorporating retrieval practice into everyday behavior. Instead of using retrieval as a method to remember information for long periods of time, students tend to rely on study practices that are not as effective, such as encoding multiple times by reading a chapter over and over. Dunlosky and colleagues (2013) found that *rereading*, a process of encoding text information multiple times, was one of the most commonly used study strategies. Unfortunately, rereading without a specific purpose and including retrieval exercises is one of the least effective study strategies. Students believe that rereading or rehearsal strategies are effective. In fact, students who use these strategies may develop what has been called the *illusion of competence* or *overconfidence problem*, illustrated in a study by Karpicke and Blunt (2011) in which students had to judge how well they learned content after using different strategies. More specifically, students were either asked to study the material once, study the material four times, study the material and create a concept map, or study and then engage in retrieval practice or free recall of the content just learned. Students who used the repeated study approach reported high levels of confidence that they had learned the content well, even though this group of students did not perform at a level consistent with these beliefs. In other words, students who engaged in repeated study thought they performed much better than they actually did perform. Perhaps most troubling about this finding is that students typically walk away from a study session feeling very confident after using the rereading approach. As a result of this overconfidence, students will stop studying sooner than they should, which can obviously lead to lower levels of academic performance. Overconfidence probably stems, at least in part, from a sense of familiarity. The more a student sees the content, the more familiar it becomes, but learning requires more than familiarity. The other interesting finding from this study was that the students who performed the best, those using retrieval practice, actually thought they were least prepared to be tested on the material (Karpicke & Blunt, 2011). In other words, students who used retrieval practice had low levels of confidence related to how well they knew the material. This means that students are not the best judges of what strategies lead to learning and may therefore not make choices that will lead to the best outcomes. This is where faculty can step in to facilitate higher levels of learning by informing students of research-based learning strategies and demonstrating the value of these strategies during class.

Informing students about the value of engaging in retrieval practice is a good first step. Many students are not aware of the testing effect and as a result may not be using this strategy. However, informing students about strategies that work may not be enough to change student behaviors. Knowledge unfortunately doesn't always lead to action. Fortunately, research has shown that when students have the opportunity to personally experience the benefit of retrieval practice, this can translate into an increased likelihood that students will use retrieval strategies (Einstein, Mullet, & Harrison, 2012). In a study by Einstein and colleagues (2012), students were asked to engage in study-study or study-test behaviors related to course content. A quiz was then distributed to assess learning. Not surprisingly, the testing effect was demonstrated, with students who used the study-test approach outperforming the students using the study-study approach. The professor displayed the class data and emphasized the importance of using retrieval practice as a learning strategy. At the end of the semester, students were surveyed about their use of study strategies. After participating in this demonstration, students reported being much more likely to use retrieval practice strategies. Specifically, 82% of the students indicated that they were much more likely to use testing as a study technique (Einstein et al., 2012). Based on this research, faculty should find ways to demonstrate the value of retrieval practice.

We can emphasize the importance of retrieval practice by providing ample opportunities for students to engage in retrieval practice to build and strengthen their memory. Quizzes are an excellent way to accomplish this goal and facilitate high-level learning. Shifting from an exam-only approach and incorporating quizzes into our course structure can send a powerful message to our students about the importance of retrieval practice. To strengthen this message, we can explicitly share our rationale for including quizzes on our syllabus, perhaps even citing the abundant research showing that students who take quizzes better retain course content. For example, Landrum (2007) found that students who took weekly quizzes throughout the semester scored higher on the final exam compared to students who did not take weekly quizzes. Learning is further enhanced when students are provided with immediate feedback and when students have multiple opportunities to take quizzes (Dihoff, Brosvic, & Epstein, 2003; Epstein, Epstein, & Brosvic, 2001). In other words, giving students many retrieval practice opportunities and providing feedback after each attempt can help students with long-term retention of course content. Online quizzing tools typically allow you to indicate the number of attempts and control whether you want your students to receive feedback after each item or quiz.

The benefit of quizzes and other retrieval practice opportunities goes beyond strengthening neural pathways. Quizzes are an excellent example of formative assessments, which are given before or during instruction to help students learn (Woolfolk, 2013). One of the primary mechanisms for improved learning is the self-regulation process. Students who monitor their progress toward goals and make adjustments to their behaviors as needed are more likely to meet with success. Feedback from quizzes or other related formative assessments can provide students with external data about how well they are learning the content and making progress toward their goal. External data are important because they help students develop a more realistic picture of their learning progress, combating the problem of illusions of competence. Research has shown that students who engage in self-regulatory processes are more likely to meet with success (Zimmerman, 2002). We can facilitate this process by structuring our classes to include quizzes and other retrieval activities to provide students with valuable feedback about their learning progress.

Some retrieval practice opportunities occur outside class or the lecture. The availability of online quizzes, for example, allows students to benefit from multiple attempts at quizzes without using class time for this purpose. Many publishers have robust online systems with numerous practice quizzing opportunities, but students often use these tools only if required. It may therefore be important for us to require students to take online quizzes or use publisher-supplied resources outside class. Although some faculty may be concerned about grade inflation issues if we give students multiple attempts at a quiz or give credit for completing online activities, this is only an issue if we count these activities as a large portion of the final grade. On the other hand, if quizzes or other retrieval practice activities only account for a small portion of the final grade (perhaps up to 10%), then grade inflation is probably not a huge concern. Having a grade attached to the quizzes sends the message to students that retrieval practice is a valuable learning activity. Students are more likely to complete tasks that are required compared to those that are optional. Thus, if we want our students to engage in retrieval practice, it may be important for these activities to be reflected in the grading system.

Although quizzes can be given outside class, it is also important to give students an opportunity to engage in retrieval practice during class. By building in retrieval practice activities, you will help students master the content as you lecture. Students will benefit most when given the opportunity to engage in retrieval practice after each important section or chunk of information. There are many ways to adapt formal lectures to include retrieval practice. Lasry, Mazur, and Watkins (2008) developed an approach called *peer instruction* that has been shown to increase learning and decrease attrition for students at an Ivy League school and at a 2-year college (2008). With this process, the instructor lectures for 10 to 15 minutes and then pauses to ask the students a multiple-choice question. Students raise their hand to signal which of the alternatives they feel is the best response. At this point students are asked to turn to their neighbors and determine the best response in pairs. The students are then again asked to select the best response from the alternatives provided. This entire process takes only about 2 or 3 minutes of class time. Most important, students have three opportunities to retrieve information just learned. Conducting this process once or twice during a 50-minute class has been shown to improve learning significantly (Couch & Mazur, 2001).

Peer instruction is only one method for students to practice recall of information as they are learning from lecture. Socratic lectures, lecture discussions, problem-solving lectures, and interactive lectures are all variations on the lecture that incorporate practice at retrieval (Major, Harris, & Zakrajsek, 2016). Frequent retrieval during lectures strengthens neural connections, provides students with external data about their performance and learning progress, and ultimately increases learning.

Retrieval practice opportunities can also be quite helpful to faculty. Brief, frequent retrieval practice exercises and quizzes can give us valuable information about how well our students are learning the course content. We can use this information as we reflect on what worked well and where we can make improvements. The feedback we receive through these retrieval activities will most certainly help us determine where and when adjustments to our teaching are needed. On the one hand, if students have difficulty on a quiz, we can provide additional examples and explanations to increase student learning. On the other hand, if students do well on a quiz, it provides us with evidence that students had success with learning that content and are ready for new content. It is much more effective for us to know if students are struggling to understand a concept early in the semester rather than waiting until after they take a major exam. Faculty using this approach will likely see higher exam grades because students are more engaged in the learning process and retrieval practice strengthens their memories.

LEARNING AND ENGAGEMENT STRATEGIES

Retrieval is much more than a mechanism to determine whether an individual has learned something new or can still remember something from long ago. The process of retrieving is an important part of the learning process and can be promoted during a lecture. The following strategies are designed to assist you in helping students practice at retrieval. If you already use some of these lecture enhancement strategies, think of ways to adapt them for future use.

Traditional Quizzes

Used at the beginning of class, quizzes can help students retrieve content learned during the previous class lecture or from the assigned readings. Quizzes can also be administered during a short break in a lecture or at the end of a class to help students build strong memories for new content. Although quizzes can be as brief as one or two questions, a variety of formats can be used for quizzing, ranging from objective true-or-false or multiple-choice tests to open-ended short answers or even brief essays. Regardless of the method, it is important for students to receive timely feedback. If possible, provide students with the answers immediately after they take the quiz. This can easily be accomplished by displaying the correct answers on a slide when using objective quizzes or verbally sharing the correct answers. For open-ended quizzes, you can spend a few minutes discussing the correct answer, or you can ask students to give their responses and then indicate whether a response was accurate. The advantage of grading a quiz, especially one that targets previously learned content, is that students will be more likely to study that content, further enhancing the learning process. The pop quiz has often been used as a way to encourage regular study habits, but students often have a negative view of this type of quiz, probably stemming from teachers or professors using the pop quiz when they suspect students did not complete reading or other assignments. In other words, the pop quiz is sometimes used in a punitive way. Ruscio (2001) found a creative way around the negative perceptions of the pop quiz by tossing a coin at the beginning of class. If it is heads, he gives a one-question short-answer quiz; if it is tails, there is no quiz that day. His students considered this approach to the pop quiz fair and therefore viewed it more positively. The advantage, of course, is that students have to prepare for every class, but the professor only has to grade quizzes about half the time. It may not always be appropriate to grade a quiz. For instance, most quizzes administered during a class on new content are not graded because this may give an unfair advantage to students who are able to more quickly process information.

Clicker or Polling Quizzes

One way to encourage retrieval practice within a class lecture through quizzing is by using clickers or polling techniques. Some colleges or classes require students to purchase clickers. In other cases, professors may be able to access clickers through their media services department. However, many other free polling options are available such as Poll Everywhere and Kahoot!. Both of these options require the use of mobile devices and access to the Internet. There are several advantages of using technology for quizzing purposes. It reduces the amount of time you need during class to distribute and collect paper quizzes. In addition, polling software allows you to display not only the correct responses but also how the class responded. This provides you and your students with real-time data about how well they are learning the content. This information can allow you to make immediate adjustments to the lecture and can also prompt students to change their learning behaviors if needed. Of course some polling options do not require any technology. You can distribute colored index cards, for instance with each color representing true or false or a, b, c, or d. When using this approach, students simply raise the card that corresponds with their answer. Regardless of the approach you use for polling, this technique encourages the use of retrieval practice and therefore will strengthen memory.

Interactive Quizzes

Although we typically think of the quiz as an independent learning activity, quizzes can also be completed in small groups either prior to a lecture to encourage students to come prepared or after a lecture to reinforce concepts just learned. With the focused interactive learning technique, students work independently on quiz questions and then work in a small group before submitting their responses (Harton et al., 2002). In this approach, students help one another retrieve and learn the content while completing the quiz. Research shows that students using this interactive quiz approach perform better compared to students who did not have the opportunity to work with others on the quiz. Students also performed better on test items related to chapters where interactive quizzes were used compared to items from chapters where interactive quizzes were not used (Harton et al., 2002). Because learning is a social activity, it makes sense that interactive quizzes are beneficial and effective. You can either provide students with the quiz questions, or you can ask students to create questions and then exchange their questions with another group. Incorporating brief, interactive quizzes can be a way to further enhance learning.

Flashcards

Good old-fashioned flashcards are excellent for promoting retrieval practice. Writing concepts on one side of an index card and the definition or explanation of the concept on the other side sets the stage for students to engage in retrieval practice and test their knowledge. During class lectures, you can encourage students to create flashcards of the most important concepts presented in class. Students can work on this independently or together to create the flashcards. Either way, it is important for all students to have full access to this study tool after class so they can practice retrieving the content. Flashcards are not just for definitions. Students can also use flashcards to help them engage in higher-level cognitive tasks. For instance, one side of the card could display an open-ended question with the answer to the question on the other side of the card. You may want to provide questions related to the lecture segment and then give students a few minutes to write their answers on the back of an index card. It is best if students complete this task without using their notes and textbook so that they engage in retrieval practice even while creating the cards. However, students will need to confirm that their responses are accurate so that they spend their time studying accurate content. There are a variety of ways you can use the flashcards during lecture pauses. In addition to having students create the flashcards, you could also have students test themselves or each other using flashcards they already created. A common practice is to put aside the cards with concepts that students believe they have already mastered, giving them more time to focus on the concepts not yet mastered. However, you may want to caution students against this practice as research has found this often results in poorer performance (Kornell & Bjork, 2008). The most likely explanation for this finding is that by putting cards aside, students are not benefitting from the repeated retrieval practice on those concepts. It is therefore best for students to test themselves on all the flashcards multiple times. Many technology tools are available to help create electronic flashcards. Many of these technology flashcard options offer students the ability to share flashcards they have created. For example, with Quizlet, an open source flashcard and testing tool, students can cocreate or share study resources. To promote collaborative studying behaviors, you may want to consider using pauses during lectures as opportunities for students to create online flashcards that will be accessible to the entire class. If you use this approach, you may want to use some of the lecture pauses for students to check the accuracy of the flashcard content. In other words, the first lecture pause could be for each small group to create a few flashcards related to the content just covered, the next pause could be used for groups to check the accuracy of another group's flashcards, and then the next or final pause could allow students to quiz one another using the cocreated flashcards. Some tools such as Quizlet allow students to turn their flashcards into practice quizzes, which is an added bonus. In other words, by creating the electronic flashcards, you are providing the online site with enough information to automatically generate quiz questions that can be helpful for studying.

Choral Responses

A very brief technique that uses retrieval practice, the choral response involves asking a question of the class as a whole at breaks within a lecture and expecting everyone in the class to answer the question together. This will obviously only work for brief one- or two-word answers. This technique could be used to help students master some basic concepts but is probably not the best choice for more complex concepts or tasks requiring critical thinking skills. An example of the choral response is asking students to name the person associated with a theory you just described. This very brief activity helps students access information previously learned, helps keep students focused and attentive during class, and provides you with information about how many of the students have grasped the theory or concept (Woolfolk, 2013).

Brief Presentations

Asking students to give a mini lecture on content previously learned is a great way for students to benefit from two incredibly powerful learning approaches: retrieval practice and teaching others. Ask students to come to class prepared to give a two-minute summary of key concepts learned from the previous class and then randomly select a student to give this mini presentation. To maximize retrieval practice, ask students to do this without notes or slides. This brief, informal presentation helps encourage students to study prior to class and then recall this information during class. The mini lecture can also take place individually or in small groups during class or at the end of a lecture.

One-Page Summaries

Asking students to create a one-page summary of the lecture is another effective way to promote retrieval practice. For this exercise, give students time at the end of class (about 5 to 10 minutes) and ask them to summarize the most important points. For students to benefit from retrieval practice, they will need to complete this activity from memory and not use their notes. For added benefit, you can ask students to create a concept map or matrix rather than just a bulleted list. This approach to the one-page summary will help students focus on not only the most important concepts but also the relationships and connections among the concept. It is important for students to confirm that their summary is accurate and on target, which can be accomplished by your reviewing the key concepts, having students compare their summaries with those completed by classmates, or having students compare their summary to their notes and textbook.

SUMMARY

Retrieval is one of the most powerful ways to learn and retain new information. There are many strategies to help students to practice engaging in retrieval before, during, and after information is presented by any type of lecture. Students may work individually, in pairs, or in small groups. The overall goal with respect to retrieval is to strengthen the pathways to the information by repeatedly using those pathways.

REFERENCES

Atkinson, R. C., & Shiffrin, R. M. (1968). Human memory: A proposed system and its control processes. In K. W. Spence, & J. T. Spence, *The psychology of learning and motivation (Vol. 2,* pp. 89–195). New York, NY: Academic Press.

Brown, P. C., Roediger, H. L., McDaniel, M. A. (2014). *Make it stick: The science of successful learning.* Cambridge, MA: Belknap Press of Harvard University Press.

Couch, C. H., & Mazur, E. (2001). Peer instruction: Ten years of experience and results. *American Journal of Physics, 69,* 970–977. doi:http://dx.doi.org/10.1119/1.1374249

Dihoff, R. E., Brosvic, G. M. & Epstein, M. L. (2003). The role of feedback during academic testing: The delay retention effect revisited. *Psychological Report, 53,* 533–548.

Doyle, T. D., & Zakrajsek, T. D. (2013). *The new science of learning: How to learn in harmony with your brain.* Sterling, VA: Stylus.

Dunlosky, J., Rawson, K. A., Marsh, E. J., Nathan, M. J., & Willingham, D. T. (2013). Improving students' learning with effective learning techniques: Promising directions from cognitive and educational psychology. *Psychological Science in the Public Interest, 14*(1), 4–58. doi:10.1177/1529100612453266

Einstein, G. O., Mullet, H. G., & Harrison, T. L. (2012). The testing effect: Illustrating a fundamental concept and changing study strategies. *Teaching of Psychology, 39,* 190–193.

Epstein, M. L., Epstein, B. B., & Brosvic, G. M. (2001). Immediate feedback during academic testing. *Psychological Reports, 88,* 889–895.

Harton, H. C., Richardson, D. S., Barreras, R. E., Rockloff, M. J., & Latané, B. (2002). Focused interactive learning: A tool for active class discussion. *Teaching of Psychology, 29,* 10–15. doi:10.1207/S15328023TOP2901_03

Karpicke, J. D., & Blunt, J. R. (2011). Retrieval practice produces more learning than elaborative studying with concept mapping. *Science, 331*, 772–775.

Karpicke, J. D., & Roediger, H. L., III. (2007). Repeated retrieval during learning is the key to long-term retention. *Journal of Memory and Language, 57*, 151–162. doi:10.1016/j.jml.2006.09.004

Kornell, N., & Bjork, R. A. (2008). Optimising self-regulated study: The benefits and costs of dropping flashcards. *Memory, 16*, 125–136. doi:10.1080/09658210701763899

Landrum, R. (2007). Introductory psychology student performance: Weekly quizzes followed by a cumulative final exam. *Teaching of Psychology, 34*, 177–180. doi:10.1080/00986280701498566

Lasry, N., Mazur, E., & Watkins, J. (2008). Peer instruction: From Harvard to the two-year college. *American Journal of Physics Teachers, 76*, 1066–1069. doi:http://dx.doi.org/10.1119/1.2978182

Logan, J. M., Thompson, A. J., & Marshak, D. W. (2011). Testing to enhance retention in human anatomy. *Anatomical Sciences Education, 4*, 243–248.

Major, C. H., Harris, M. S., & Zakrajsek, T. (2016). *Teaching for learning: 101 intentionally designed educational activities to put students on the path to success.* New York, NY: Routledge.

Meyer, A. D., & Logan, J. M. (2013). Taking the testing effect beyond the college freshman: Benefits for lifelong learning. *Psychology and Aging, 28*, 142–147. doi:10.1037/a0030890

Myers, D. G. (2014). *Exploring psychology* (8th ed.). New York, NY: Worth.

Roediger, H. I., Agarwal, P. K., McDaniel, M. A., & McDermott, K. B. (2011). Test-enhanced learning in the classroom: Long-term improvements from quizzing. *Journal of Experimental Psychology: Applied, 17*, 382–395. doi:10.1037/a0026252

Roediger, H. L., & Karpicke, J. D. (2006a). The power of testing memory: Basic research and implications for educational practice. *Perspectives on Psychological Science, 1*, 181–210. doi:10.1111/j.1745-6916.2006.00012.x

Roediger, H. L., & Karpicke, J. D. (2006b). Test-enhanced learning: Taking memory tests improves long-term retention. *Psychological Science, 17*, 249–255. doi:10.1111/j.1467-9280.2006.01693.x

Ruscio, J. (2001). Administering quizzes at random to increase students' reading. *Teaching of Psychology, 28*, 204–206. doi:10.1207/S15328023TOP2803_08

Woolfolk, A. (2013). *Educational psychology* (12th ed.). Boston, MA: Pearson Education.

Zimmerman, B. J. (2002). Becoming a self-regulated learner: An overview. *Theory into Practice, 41*(2), 64–72.

9

QUESTIONING FOR CRITICAL THINKING

QUESTIONS ARE POWERFUL LEARNING tools. According to Larson and Lovelace (2013), "Although advances in technology and pedagogical methods are changing the ways in which teachers teach, basic question-and-answer approaches continue to be a fundamentally important aspect of instruction in modern college classrooms" (p. 105). Bain (2004) believes questions serve to organize our course content and draw student attention to the most important concepts. In other words, questions can have a cueing effect, alerting students that the content related to the question asked is important (Gall, 1984). Questions also provide students with an opportunity to retrieve previously stored information and can play an important role in developing critical thinking skills (Woolfolk, 2013).

The questioning technique has long been used to increase comprehension of course-related content inside and outside the classroom. For example, educators have often encouraged students to use questioning strategies when reading and learning from textbooks and when listening to lectures. Research has shown that reading techniques that incorporate questioning approaches such as SQ3R (discussed in Chapter 4) have been linked to higher levels of reading comprehension and exam performance (Artis, 2008; Carlston, 2011). For the questioning component of this technique, students are taught to consider questions posed by the author or to generate questions based on a survey or preview of the chapter before they begin reading the chapter. As they read, students are more actively engaged with the text because they are looking for answers to these questions, and this shifts reading from a passive to an active process. In essence, the questions can help students focus on the most important content of the chapter and give purpose to the reading activity. The questioning technique can also be easily incorporated into our lectures. Bain (2015) suggests we use questions to frame our lectures and to increase student learning.

The two main types of questions are lower level, or factual, questions and higher level, or critical thinking, questions. We can use Bloom's (1956) taxonomy to help us differentiate between the lower and the higher level questions. The six levels of knowing from lowest to highest are remembering, understanding, applying, analyzing, evaluating, and creating (Anderson & Krathwohl, 2001; Bloom, 1956). Questions that tap into the remembering or understanding levels are typically factual or lower level questions that often have simple or straightforward responses. Questions such as, "What is the name of the theory or concept?" or "Can you list the three major components of the model?" are examples of factual, low-level questions. Questions that ask students to engage in application, analysis, evaluation, and creation are examples of higher level cognitive questions. Questions tapping into these higher cognitive tasks promote critical thinking, encouraging students to think more deeply about the content. Questions such as, "How does this theory compare to and contrast with to the theory we discussed last week?" "What would be the best course of action in this situation?" and "How can this information be used to create a new product?" are examples of higher level questions. Research has found that both types of questions can increase learning, although, not surprisingly, higher level cognitive questions tend to result in higher levels of achievement (Gall, 1984). King (1995) argues that the level of question directly influences the level of learning, meaning high-level questions are needed to promote high-level thinking. One way questions promote high-level thinking is by creating a cognitive conflict. For instance, if a question challenges a currently held belief, it may lead to a change in how students think about the content. Although critical thinking questions are important, this doesn't mean that lower level questions are not valuable. On the contrary, factual, low-level questions can help students build basic foundational knowledge in your discipline, setting the stage for critical thinking skills to develop. A strong foundational knowledge in the subject matter is needed to effectively engage in tasks that require critical thinking (Anderson & Krathwohl, 2001; Bers et al., 2015; Fink, 2003).

What type of questions do professors typically ask in discussion lectures and other forms of lectures? In a fascinating study, Larson and Lovelace (2013) investigated the questioning technique in the college classroom. Researchers observed 18 classes taught by 4 different professors. On average, professors asked about 15 questions for each 50-minute lecture. The majority of questions were factual or low level. Specifically, 78% of the questions targeted the remembering and understanding levels of Bloom's (1956) taxonomy, whereas only 4.7% of the questions targeted the evaluating and creating levels. This result is consistent with other research findings that convergent questions, factual questions with a correct response, are the type of question most often asked during lectures (Jiang, 2014). As the question-asking process for factual questions takes much less time than it does for critical thinking questions, it makes sense that factual questions would be more frequently asked. However, it is important to ask not only lower level questions but also higher level questions. If we want to build critical thinking skills in our students, incorporating critical thinking questions into our lectures will help us achieve this goal. Socratic questions are often used to help students with clarification, challenge assumptions, explore various perspectives or evidence, connect content to real-world scenarios, and promote self-reflection. The following are some examples of Socratic questions, based on the work of Paul (1990) and Strang (2011):

- What do you mean by . . .?
- What are the potential advantages and disadvantages of . . .?
- What other explanations might account for this?
- What are the assumptions behind this statement?
- What additional evidence can you find to support or refute this idea?
- What are the potential consequences of this action?
- What is the importance of learning about this topic?

Many students do not voluntarily respond to questions posed during lectures. We've probably all experienced asking a question during a lecture and being faced with silence and blank stares. Based on research reviewed by Weaver and Qi (2005), only about 25% of college students voluntarily respond to questions. Research has found that student participation drops more as class size increases (Kenney & Banerjee, 2011). Most students opt out of voluntarily answering questions for many different reasons.

The nature of the question can play an important role in whether students will answer the question. Students may be less willing to take a risk and answer a question when it seems that the professors are looking for a very specific response. This is the case with convergent questions that only have one right answer (Woolfolk, 2013). Only the most confident students will be willing to voluntarily answer a convergent question. Students who may know the correct answer but are not sure if their response is the one the instructor is looking for will likely opt out of volunteering a response. Students may also choose not to respond if they perceive the answer to be obvious or too easy (Kenney & Banerjee, 2011). However, if students believe there are several acceptable responses, as is the case with divergent questions, they are more likely to raise their hand and provide a response (Woolfolk, 2013). Divergent questions not only encourage higher levels of student participation but also are more likely to promote critical thinking skills (Jiang, 2014). It is therefore important for us to ask divergent, high-level questions. Larson and Lovelace (2013) suggest that professors carefully consider the learning goals of the lecture as they craft their questions. In other words, it is important for questions to be well-thought-out components of the lecture that tap into foundational knowledge and critical thinking goals of the course.

One reason students may not respond could be that we don't give them enough time. Students need adequate time to process the question and find an answer. Classic research has shown that K–12 teachers wait only about one second after asking a question before continuing with the lesson (Rowe, 1972). A study investigating wait time in the college classroom found that the average wait time was 3.75 seconds (Larson & Lovelace, 2013). Although 1 to 3 seconds does not sound very long, it can feel like an eternity when standing in front of a class where no one is volunteering to participate. Our short wait times are probably because of the uncomfortable feeling we experience when standing in front of a silent room. However, we need to remember that it takes time for students to process the question and recall the necessary information before providing a response. The amount of time we need to give should vary based on the complexity of the question. Simpler questions will obviously require less time than cognitively challenging questions. Interestingly, research shows that professors do not typically adjust their wait time based on question complexity (Larson & Lovelace, 2013). Determining how much wait time is needed should become a part of our planning process.

Rowe (1972) found that increasing wait time by just three to five seconds after posing a question had many positive benefits such as increased student responses and longer, more in-depth responses. Larson and Lovelace (2013) suggest that college professors should wait four to six seconds after asking a question. They also suggest advising students to write down their response before verbally responding, noting that this strategy can lead to stronger responses. When students are writing their response, the thinking time or period of silence is easier for professors to tolerate because they can see that the students are actively engaged in a task. An additional benefit of having students write their answer before verbally responding is that this strategy cognitively engages all students in the class and not just the few students who may volunteer to respond to the question. Research has found that student participation in whole-class discussions increases when students have an opportunity to think about and discuss responses with a peer. This was illustrated in a study by Rocca (2010), who found that

> confidence gained by advanced preparation helps to counteract classroom apprehension, as evidenced by the fact that students who were allowed to talk about the topic with another student or to complete it as a homework assignment before discussing it with the entire class were more likely to participate. (p. 192)

Often, increasing wait time is not enough. The classroom climate also plays an important role in whether students will be willing to take a risk and voluntarily respond to questions. For example, faculty can create a classroom climate that encourages student participation and increases the likelihood that students will voluntarily respond to questions by knowing students' names; arranging the chairs in a circle when possible; and treating all students with respect, especially when reacting to their responses.

To be inclusive and to avoid having the same students answering all the questions all the time, many professors randomly call on students, which is often referred to as the *cold call*. The intent behind this approach is to increase the attention and engagement of all students throughout the lecture. White (2011), however, asks faculty to carefully consider this practice, stating that faculty need to be "aware that silence represents far more than a student's lack of interest, knowledge, or desire to participate" (p. 262). Because of linguistic and cultural issues, some students may not be comfortable answering questions in front of the class, especially in larger classes. Other reasons students don't voluntarily participate include being concerned about negative reactions from the professor and peers and not believing they know the correct answer because of difficulty understanding the course content (Kenney & Banerjee, 2011). If we opt to use the cold call, it is important for us to clearly communicate expectations, give students processing time, and maybe give them the option of passing or not responding. In addition, to avoid unintentional bias when selecting students to participate, using a true random process is important, and technology tools such as apps can be used for this purpose. Research shows that faculty may unintentionally treat students differently; for example, Rocca (2010) reviewed research that showed that professors treat males and females differently.

Researchers have found that randomly calling on students has been connected to increased learning because students are more likely to come to class prepared (Dallimore, Hertenstein, & Platt, 2004). However, many professors worry about the anxiety students may experience when this approach is used. Martino and Sala (1996) found that most students in a large lecture class where the professor used the cold call technique responded positively. It is important to note, however, that students responded more favorably to critical thinking questions than factual ones, which they perceived as oral quizzes. It should be noted that in this study, students were given time to process the question before communicating an answer and were also allowed to pass if they did not want to respond. It is possible that students would have had a more negative experience if these strategies were not incorporated into the cold call technique.

According to the results of a large-scale study of more than 1,500 undergraduate and graduate students, Weaver and Qi (2005) found that the faculty-student relationship outside class was the best predictor of whether students voluntarily participated during class. Specifically, it was found "that among 10 causal variables studied, *faculty-student interaction* seems to have the largest direct, indirect, and total effects on participation as reported by students" (Weaver & Qi, 2005, p. 591). A huge body of literature has shown that faculty-student relationships play an extremely important role in learning and overall success (Micari & Pazos, 2012; Woodside, Wong, & Weist, 1999). Based on these findings, we need to remember that our interactions with students outside the classroom can affect dynamics during lectures and other in-class learning activities. Building relationships with students outside class is therefore important. However, we need to keep in mind that some students may be more likely to initiate interactions with us outside the classroom. Weaver and Qi (2005), for instance, found that females and nontraditional-age students were more likely to visit professors during office hours than were males and traditional-age students. Knowing this information, we may need to be the ones who initiate interactions with our students outside the classroom setting so all our students are able to benefit.

After a question is asked and answered, we need to react or respond to provide students with important feedback and either encourage or inhibit further participation. Woolfolk (2013) suggests positively reinforcing correct answers with a clear statement that the response is accurate and sometimes adding a further explanation of why the answer was on target. This becomes an opportunity for us to elaborate on student responses, making additional connections among concepts. When an answer is incorrect, we can ask more questions to assist the student with answering the question correctly. For example, we could provide clues or remind students about related content, in essence, supporting students when they are working on finding appropriate responses. It is important to clearly but respectfully indicate when responses are incorrect. Being unclear about which responses are accurate or inaccurate can hinder the learning process. Providing this sort of feedback in a respectful, supportive manner increases the likelihood that students will participate again in the future (Rocca, 2010). This is particularly important because one of the primary reasons students do not want to respond to questions is fear of a negative response from faculty or peers (Kenney & Banerjee, 2011).

Although most of us think of questioning as a technique for professors, students can take on the role of questioner. To teach students how to become effective questioners, King (1995) suggests providing students with generic question stems such as, "What is the difference between ____ and _____?" "What would happen if _______?" and "How does _____ tie in with what we learned before?" (p. 14). At lecture pauses, she asks students to use the generic question stems to develop a question or two related to the content just learned and then has students discuss their questions in small groups. Research by King (1991) shows that teaching students how to effectively engage in questioning has academic benefits. In this study that investigated whether self-questioning during lectures increased learning, 56 ninth-grade honor students were randomly assigned to one of the following groups: self-questioning only, self-questioning with reciprocal peer questioning, discussion, and independent review. All students were given a pretest, immediate posttest, and delayed posttest (10 days later). Students in the self-questioning groups received 90 minutes of training on how to develop high-level questions. The students in the self-questioning with reciprocal peer-questioning group had to ask one another the questions they created. Although there were no differences between the groups on the pretest, students in the self-questioning and self-questioning and reciprocal peer questioning groups significantly outperformed students in the discussion and independent review groups on the immediate and delayed posttest.

Although we have primarily been focusing on questioning during the lecture, questions can also be used outside class. Adrian (2010) found that students who answered online questions about the course content demonstrated higher levels of learning. Students reported that answering the online questions helped them synthesize information and required them to revisit their notes. In other words, the online discussion questions set the stage for increased learning. Guiller, Durndell, and Ross (2008) found that critical thinking skills were more likely to develop through online conversations compared to traditional in-class discussions. This is probably because of the time that students have to think and process the question and gather information before responding to the question prompt. One way to facilitate higher level conversations during class is to begin the conversation in the online environment so that students have time to think about the question. In class, the conversation can be extended, giving students an opportunity to dive even deeper into the content.

LEARNING AND ENGAGEMENT STRATEGIES

Asking good questions and having students respond is an essential part of any good educational experience. Integrating good questions and discussion into the lecture should not be seen as merely a break from the lecture, but rather an integral part of the lecture to check for understanding and to reinforce newly learned material. The following strategies are designed to assist you in helping students to better learn through participation. If you already use some of these lecture enhancement strategies, think of ways to adapt them for future use.

Set the Tone

Before you begin asking questions prior to or during a lecture, it is essential to create a supportive learning environment. A primary reason students avoid answering questions during class is fear of disapproval by the professor or peers (Kenney & Banerjee, 2011), so it is not likely students will take a risk in a nonsupportive environment. Interacting with students in a respectful way in and out of the classroom will help you facilitate a productive learning environment where students are willing to take risks and be more engaged. Explaining the rationale behind our teaching approaches can also contribute to a positive classroom culture. For example, we can share research that shows that student participation is linked to increased learning.

Quick Comprehension Checks

Asking low-level or factual questions during the lecture can be a great way to maintain student attention, give students the chance to engage in retrieval practice, and obtain immediate feedback about how well students are understanding the content. These quick questions can be in the form of a verbal shout out where all students must answer the question simultaneously or could be posed to the entire class and the instructor waits for someone to respond. It is challenging to assess whether students are understanding the material when you pose the question to the class as a whole and rely on volunteers because you won't know if everyone is grasping the content. Thus, you may opt to use a cold call approach to randomly sample the class; technology apps can be used for this purpose. With most of the apps, you can either enter the names of all the students in your class and then click on the button to randomly select a name, or you can use an app that randomly selects a number, put a number next to all the student's names on your roster, and then call on the student corresponding to the number selected. A no-tech option is to have an index card for each student (some faculty like to ask students to write down a few facts about themselves on an index card on the first day of class) and then shuffle and select a card. Given some of the concerns discussed previously about the cold call, you may want to first give students a few minutes to think independently then discuss their thoughts with a classmate before you randomly ask students to answer a question. Polling is another option that allows you to quickly ask a comprehension-check question. The advantage of this approach is that all students are involved, and the class scores can be displayed on the screen.

Reading Assignment Questions

One way to facilitate higher level thinking is to ask questions based on an assignment students have already completed. Reading assignments work great for this purpose. Giving students questions to answer about the chapter or other readings ahead of time can not only increase their reading comprehension but also increase the likelihood of a more substantive and meaningful discussion in class. At the beginning of class, students can work with a partner to discuss their responses. While they are engaged in this process, you can walk around the room spot-checking their responses and if desired assigning a grade for the assignment. During class, you can pause at different points of the lecture and ask students to answer questions related to the content you just covered. Because students had an opportunity to discuss the questions at the beginning of class, they will be ready for random calling during the class period. If you do not want to use the beginning of class time for students to review their reading assignments with a partner, you can pause after each lecture segment and have students discuss the questions related to that portion of the lecture with a partner or small group. During this time, you can move around the classroom, listening to their responses. This will help you determine if students are fully comprehending the content. You may then want to review the questions and answers as a whole class, although it is not necessary to always engage in a large-group discussion after small-group work.

Lecture Outcome Questions

As Bain (2015) suggested, we can use questions to frame our lectures. Providing students with questions prior to a lecture can help students focus on what is most important. When students are searching for the answers to questions, they will be more cognitively engaged. Questions can make the purpose of the lecture more visible and explicit. After you determine the two or three most important learning outcomes for each lecture, rephrase the outcomes as questions, which can be put on the syllabus or displayed on the screen at the start of class. At the end of class, you can ask students to independently answer the questions and then review their responses with a classmate.

Critical Thinking Questions

As we plan our lectures, we should consider how questions promote high levels of learning. Although many of the questions we ask may naturally evolve as a result of class activities and discussions, posing a few questions that are directly connected to our learning outcomes for the day is advisable. Engaging in this planning process will increase the likelihood of incorporating high-level critical thinking questions into our lectures. These more cognitively complex questions will also take more class time, adding to the importance of planning. Creating effective question prompts can be challenging. We can use Bloom's taxonomy as a guide for our question development, identifying questions that require students to apply, analyze, evaluate, and create (Anderson & Krathwohl, 2001). Socratic questions can also be used to help promote critical thinking skills. Socratic questions may work well as the initial question prompt but are also very valuable tools for getting students to dive deeper into the content. For example, after a student responds to a question, asking additional questions such as, "What other explanations might there be?" or "What is the impact of this finding?" enhances the learning process because it helps students challenge and extend their thinking. When using high-level questions, it is important to allot enough time for students to think about the question and respond. Asking students to write down their response before verbally sharing their thoughts will lead to more substantive and thoughtful dialogues. To engage all students, rely more heavily on small-group discussions rather than the whole class discussion, although it will sometimes be important to summarize the key points with the entire class.

Peer Questioning

As noted by King (1991), students can also be the questioners. Instead of providing questions for students to answer, we can train students to develop effective questions. Providing models of generic question stems can be incredibly helpful to help students learn how to develop high-level questions. Using generic question stems that are aligned with Socratic questioning techniques will be more likely to elicit critical thinking skills. During lecture pauses, we can then ask students to generate questions about the course content, and these student-created questions can be used for small- or large-group discussions.

Online Discussions

Learning must extend beyond the classroom walls. Research has shown that online discussions promote critical thinking skills (Adrian, 2011; Guiller et al., 2008). Online discussions are at the heart of most online classes, but they can also be used as an additional learning tool in traditional classes. Online discussion boards can be used to get a conversation started prior to class or to continue conversations that began during class. In other words, online discussions should not be viewed as separate from the lecture but rather should be incorporated into the overall learning experience. Professors can make references to points made by students in the online forum as they lecture, for example, by highlighting an effective example from the online discussion. In addition, we can challenge statements and ask follow-up questions during class.

Corners

O'Connor (2013) described a physical way for students to answer questions by using the corners technique in which students move to a predesignated corner of the room that corresponds to a specific response to a question. This technique requires providing students with four answer options. Although this approach probably works best for opinion-based questions, there are ways to use this approach to promote more sophisticated thinking during a discussion lecture. You can encourage students to move beyond opinions and work with classmates to look for data or evidence that either supports or negates their initial opinion. Another option is to ask the students in each corner to work from a different perspective. In other words, students may agree with the Corner A response, but now they have to defend the Corner B response. This activity can promote higher level critical thinking skills, but it is important to note that it can require a significant amount of class time depending on the nature of the questions and corresponding activities.

Brain Writing

Brain writing is an activity that promotes creativity and high-level thought (Heslin, 2009; Paulus & Yang, 2000). To engage students in the brainwriting process, assign students to small groups and distribute index cards to each of them. Next, ask students to write down their response to a question you ask. After students have an opportunity to write down one response, they should pass the index card to their right. At this point, they should have an index card in front of them that has one response to your question. Students now need to add another response but cannot use the response they already wrote down and cannot use the idea that is already on the index card. Repeat this process until the cards get back to the original student, or it seems that students are really struggling to find other answers. During this part of the process, students should not discuss any of the ideas with other students. For the next part of the process, students discuss all the responses with the other members of their group. The act of brain writing before discussion typically results in more ideas and is an easy way to be sure the ideas of all participants are a part of the conversation, which can be drawn into the next part of the lecture. Although this strategy works well for question prompts that target creativity, it can also be used for students to review content. For example, asking, "What were the most important concepts of the lecture?" could serve as the question prompt before students engage in brain writing.

SUMMARY

Of the multiple types of lectures that exist, those that include student responses to questions and class discussions are consistently shown to be the most effective. The strategies provided in this chapter are designed to help make student participation a regular part of the course and effectively integrated into lectures. The overall goal with respect to student participation is to help students practice critical thinking and become more sophisticated consumers of information.

REFERENCES

Adrian, L. M. (2010). Active learning in large classes: Can small interventions produce greater results than are statistically predictable? *JGE: The Journal of General Education*, 59, 223–237. doi:10.1353/jge.2010.0024

Anderson, L. & Krathwohl, D. A. (2001) *Taxonomy for learning, teaching and assessing: A revision of Bloom's taxonomy of educational objectives*. New York, NY: Longman.

Artis, A. B. (2008). Improving marketing students' reading comprehension with the SQ3R method. *Journal of Marketing Education, 30*, 130–137.

Bain, K. (2004). *What the best teachers do*. Cambridge, MA: Harvard University Press.

Bain, K. (2015., August). *Deep learning.* Presented at the meeting of Engaging Learners in the 21st Century, Mercer County Community College, West Windsor, NJ.

Bers, T., Chun, M., Daly, W. T., Harrington, C., Toblowsky, B. F., & Associates. (2015). *Foundations for critical thinking.* Columbia: University of South Carolina, National Resource Center for the First-Year Experience and Students in Transition.

Bloom, B. S. (Ed.). (1956). *Taxonomy of educational objectives: The classification of educational goals; Handbook I: Cognitive domain.* White Plains, NY: Longmans, Green.

Carlston, D. L. (2011). Benefits of student-generated note packets: A preliminary investigation of SQ3R implementation. *Teaching of Psychology, 38*, 142–146.

Dallimore, E. J., Hertenstein, J. H., & Platt, M. B. (2004). Classroom participation and discussion effectiveness: Student-generated strategies. *Communication Education, 53*(1), 103–115.

Fink, L. (2003). *Creating significant learning experiences: An integrated approach to designing college courses.* San Francisco, CA: Jossey-Bass.

Gall, M. (1984). Synthesis of research on teachers' questioning. *Educational Leadership, 42*(3), 40–48.

Guiller, J., Durndell, A., & Ross, A. (2008). Peer interaction and critical thinking: Face-to-face or online discussion? *Learning and Instruction*, 18, 187–200.

Heslin, P. A. (2009). Better than brainstorming? Potential contextual boundary conditions to brainwriting for idea generation in organizations. *Journal of Occupational and Organizational Psychology*, 82, 129–145. doi:10.1348/096317908X285642

Jiang, Y. (2014). Exploring teacher questioning as a formative assessment strategy. *RELC Journal*, 45, 287–304. doi:10.1177/0033688214546962

Kenney, J. L., & Banerjee, P. (2011). "Would someone say something, please?" Increasing student participation in college classrooms. *Journal on Excellence in College Teaching, 22*(4), 57–81.

King, A. (1991). Improving lecture comprehension: Effects of a metacognitive strategy. *Applied Cognitive Psychology*, 5, 331–346.

King, A. (1995). Designing the instructional process to enhance critical thinking across the curriculum—Inquiring minds really do want to know: Using questioning to teach critical thinking. *Teaching of Psychology*, 22, 13–17.

Larson, L. R., & Lovelace, M. D. (2013). Evaluating the efficacy of questioning strategies in lecture-based classroom environments: Are we asking the right questions? *Journal on Excellence in College Teaching, 24*(1), 105–122.

Martino, G., & Sala, F. (1996). *Engaging students in large lecture classes.* Proceedings of the 10th Annual Conference on Undergraduate Teaching of Psychology, March 20–22. Ellenville, NY. Retrieved from ERIC database.

Micari, M., & Pazos, P. (2012). Connecting to the professor: Impact of the student–faculty relationship in a highly challenging course. *College Teaching, 60*(2), 41–47.

O'Connor, K. J. (2013). Class participation: Promoting in-class student engagement. *Education, 133*, 340–344.

Paul, R. (1990). *Critical thinking: What every person needs to survive in a rapidly changing world.* Rohnert Park, CA: Center for Critical Thinking and Moral Critique.

Paulus, P. B., & Yang, H. (2000). Idea generation in groups: A basis for creativity in organizations. *Organizational Behavior and Human Decision Processes, 82*(1), 76–87. doi:10.1006/obhd.2000.2888

Rocca, K. A. (2010). Student participation in the college classroom: An extended multidisciplinary literature review. *Communication Education, 59*, 185–213. doi:10.1080/03634520903505936

Rowe, M. B. (1972). *Wait-time and rewards as instructional variables: Their influence on language, logic, and fate control.* Retrieved from ERIC database. (ED061103)

Strang, K. (2011). How can discussion forum questions be effective in online MBA courses? *Campus-Wide Information Systems, 28*, 80–92.

Weaver, R. R., & Qi, J. (2005). Classroom organization and participation: College students' perceptions. *Journal of Higher Education, 76*, 570–601.

White, J. W. (2011). Resistance to classroom participation: Minority students, academic discourse, cultural conflicts, and issues of representation in whole class discussions. *Journal of Language, Identity, and Education, 10*, 250–265.

Woodside, B. M., Wong, E. H., & Weist, D. J. (1999). The effect of student-faculty interaction on college students' academic achievement and self-concept. *Education, 119*, 730–733.

Woolfolk, A. (2013). *Educational psychology* (12th ed.). Boston, MA: Pearson Education.

PART THREE

PLANNING AND EVALUATING LECTURES

10

PLANNING EFFECTIVE LECTURES

As experts in our field, we can easily talk for hours about our disciplines. Thus, walking into a class and lecturing on a topic is a relatively easy task if our view of the lecture is simply a professor talking about her or his field of expertise. However, simply talking about our discipline is not likely to lead to student learning. Creating an effective lecture requires significant planning. Lectures are not simply conversations, they are carefully crafted lessons that help students build a solid foundational knowledge base in our field and develop critical thinking skills. When done effectively, lectures can inspire, motivate, and engage students in the learning process. To be effective, we need to be experts not only in the content of our field but also on best pedagogical practices. The teaching strategies presented throughout this book, which are based on the scholarship of teaching and learning literature, can help us transform our lectures into extremely powerful vehicles for learning.

The planning process is driven by the learning outcomes for the course. Each lecture needs to fit into the overall structure and purpose of the course, aligning with the overarching learning outcomes. In other words, we need to carefully think about how we can best use each class session to reach the course goals. When thinking about the goals for each lesson and how they relate to the overall course goals, a great place to start is to identify approximately three big ideas or most important points of each lecture. These big ideas can then be used to help you organize the lecture content and to determine how and when to incorporate active learning strategies. In other words, the learning outcomes connected to the big ideas drive the creation of the lesson plan for each lecture.

To effectively plan a lecture, it is important to consider content, delivery, and timing and sequencing. The worksheets in Appendix 10 contain lecture planning documents that can assist you with the planning process starting broadly with Section 1. Section 2 is designed to assist you in focusing on the important content of your lecture. For each big idea, write down in the space provided how the new content connects to previously learned content, what images or other multimedia tools can best assist students with learning the content, examples that best illustrate the concepts, and questions that set the stage for critical thinking. It is hoped that this document helps you organize the content of the lecture while paying special attention to lecture enhancement strategies discussed throughout this book.

As we have discussed, how we deliver the content is just as important as what content we teach. In other words, an effective lecturer will spend a considerable amount of time and energy planning how to teach the content so that students will learn the knowledge and skills associated with our discipline. Section 3 is designed to assist you with focusing on the best way to present the lecture you develop. In particular, the question prompts in this worksheet will help you consider how you can bring attention to and emphasize the big ideas or important points of the lecture. In addition, you will also want to consider what reflection and retrieval practice opportunities will best help students learn the content. Often, reflection activities incorporate retrieval practice, so having two separate activities is not critical. It may also make more sense to use a reflection or retrieval practice activity that focuses on all three of the big ideas. In other words, it is not important to provide different activities for each empty box but rather to think about your lecture as a whole and whether you are giving students the opportunity to benefit from reflection and retrieval practice for all the big ideas you are presenting. As you are working on completing these lecture planning documents, refer to Table 10.1, which provides a list of all of the lecture enhancement strategies shared throughout the book.

Section 4 focuses on timing and sequencing. Think about how you can break up the allotted time you have in a class period into lecture and active learning segments. In addition to identifying the lecture and active learning segments, consider how to best introduce the topic and also how to summarize the content at the end of the lecture. The lecture and active learning segments do not need to be equal in terms of length of time spent on each one. Some topics or activities may require more time than others. In many cases, the time spent on lecturing will be much longer than the time spent on active learning opportunities. As discussed previously, a good general rule is to incorporate some type of reflection or active learning activity after about 15 minutes of lecturing, even though we know that many factors can influence when a lecture break is needed. These breaks from the lecture could be as brief as a minute or two or could be more involved and take significantly more class time. This time line should be viewed as a guide and does not need to be adhered to in a rigid manner. It may be that the students in your class have questions or need additional explanations of concepts, and addressing these issues is important. Although plans are important, they do need to be somewhat flexible so you can be responsive to the needs of your students. In other words, plans can guide our teaching practices but we don't need to rigidly adhere to the plan; instead, expert lecturers use their plan while adapting it to the current needs of students.

APPENDIX 10: LECTURE PLANNING DOCUMENTS

INSTRUCTIONS FOR LECTURE PLANNING

Section 1: Linking Lesson to Course Goals

Effective planning begins with a focus on goals. Start by documenting the course-level learning outcomes. Next, identify a few goals or learning objectives for the lecture. Finally, write down the main topics that will be addressed during this lecture.

Section 2: Exploring Lecture Content

For each learning objective you identified, think about the best way to help students learn the related content. Consider the following:

- How does the new content connect to prior knowledge?
- What images or other multimedia tools will best help students achieve this learning objective?
- What examples will help students understand the big ideas of the lecture?
- What questions will get students thinking critically about the big ideas?

Section 3: Exploring Delivery Methods

Think about how to best infuse lecture enhancement strategies to help students achieve the learning objectives for the lecture. Refer to Table 10.1 for an overview of lecture enhancement strategies. Consider the following:

- How will you bring attention to and emphasize important points?
- What reflection exercises will best help students achieve the learning objectives?
- How will you give students an opportunity to engage in retrieval practice?

Section 4: Timing and Sequencing

Think about the sequencing of the content and how much time is needed to effectively address the big ideas of your lecture. Write a brief description of the content that you will teach in the introduction, each lecture segment, and the conclusion. Then, write a brief description of each active learning opportunity you will incorporate into the lecture. In the Time row, indicate what time you plan to start each lecture or active learning segment of the class. This will help you plan and pace the class lesson.

SECTION 1: LINKING LESSON TO COURSE GOALS

Course Learning Outcomes:

Objective(s) of the Day (Big Ideas):

Topic(s) of the Day:

SECTION 2: EXPLORING LECTURE CONTENT

Learning Objectives/ Big Ideas	How does this new content connect to prior knowledge?	What images or multimedia tools will best help students learn this big idea?	What examples will best help students understand this big idea?	What questions will get students thinking critically about this big idea?
1.				
2.				
3.				

SECTION 3: EXPLORING DELIVERY METHODS

Learning Objectives/Big Ideas	How will you bring attention to and emphasize important points?	What reflection exercises will best help students learn this big idea?	How will you give students an opportunity to engage in retrieval practice?
1.			
2.			
3.			

SECTION 4: TRANSFORMING YOUR LECTURE: FOCUS ON TIMING AND SEQUENCING

Introduction	Lecture Segment 1	Active Learning Opportunity 1	Lecture Segment 2
Content to Teach:	Content to Teach:	Description:	Content to Teach:
Time:	Time:	Time:	Time:
Active Learning Opportunity 2	**Lecture Segment 3**	**Active Learning Segment 3**	**Conclusion/Summary**
Description:	Content to Teach:	Content to Teach:	Content to Teach:
Time:	Time:	Time:	Time:

TABLE 10.1
Lecture Planning: Lecture Enhancement Strategies to Consider

Goal	Possible Strategies
Activate Prior Knowledge	Pretest Quick quizzes Dusting off the cobwebs What do I know? Turn and talk Explicit links Teach mini lesson before assigning reading
Reflection	One-minute papers Index card fast pass conversation exercise News report Concept map comparisons Think, pair, share Review and compare notes Reflective journal Tweet summaries Blogs and wikis
Capture Attention and Emphasize Important Points	Classroom culture focused on learning Address off-task behaviors Discuss detrimental effects of multitasking Identify the big ideas Use a hook, or attention getter Be passionate and use your voice Use gestures and symbols Build in active learning breaks Teach students to read and highlight effectively

(Continued)

TABLE 10.1 (*CONTINUED*)

Goal	Possible Strategies
Retrieval Practice	Traditional quizzes Clicker or polling quizzes Interactive quizzes Flashcards Choral responses Brief presentations One-page summary
Effective Use of Multimedia and Technology	Identify relevant images, graphs, or charts Create and post slides prior to lecture Ask students to find visual images related to content Use video clips to emphasize big ideas Use polling techniques Consider incorporating social media into lectures Use asynchronous chats
Questioning for Critical Thinking	Set the tone Quick comprehension checks Reading assignment questions Lecture outcome questions Critical thinking questions Peer questioning Online discussions Corners Brain writing
Make it Meaningful Through Examples	Provide two examples for each big idea Incorporate case studies Use small-group discussions of case studies Create Make it meaningful teams Think, pair, share Have students complete example tables Use a webquest

11

EVALUATING LECTURES

HOW DO WE KNOW if our lecture was effective? Because teaching and learning processes are so complex, evaluating the lecture or other teaching methods can be quite challenging. Despite this challenge, it is important to find ways to meaningfully assess our teaching practices. Determining what is and is not working well will help us make adjustments and improvements aimed at increasing student learning. A variety of informal and formal assessment approaches are available for this purpose. Reflecting on our lectures, attending to the nonverbal feedback of students during class, or listening to student comments are examples of informal approaches. Reviewing audio or video recordings of our lectures, student surveys, student performance on academic tasks, and peer observations are more formal approaches to evaluating our teaching. Teaching and learning centers are also a valuable resource, providing us with opportunities to reflect on our teaching practices.

SELF-REFLECTION

One simple yet powerful way we can improve our teaching is through reflection. Most of us will automatically review what went well and what didn't go as well as we leave class, making mental notes about what we might do differently next time. Although informal reflection is a productive activity, reflection can be even more effective when done in a more systematic, formal way. Zhao (2012) found that educators who participate in significant professional development are more likely to engage in deeper, more meaningful reflection. Incorporating reflection into the broader scope of professional development activities can be beneficial.

Keeping a reflective teaching journal can help us be more intentional as we reflect on our teaching practices. When using a journal, Titus and Gremler (2010) suggest considering whether your teaching actions were aligned with your beliefs or teaching philosophy. Journal entries may be very brief and include responses to several basic questions such as the following:

- Did my teaching actions match my teaching philosophy?
- What went well today?
- How could I improve this lecture?
- What letter grade would I give myself on the quality of my teaching today?

Journals could also be much more specific and comprehensive, addressing question prompts such as the following:

- How well did I grab the attention of my students?
- How well did I communicate the main ideas for the lecture?
- How well did assignments or previous learning tasks prepare students for the lecture?
- Was I able to effectively activate students' relevant prior knowledge?
- How effective were my examples?
- Did my media tools support student learning?
- Did the lecture enhancements or brief active learning opportunities help students master the content?
- When were students most engaged?
- What concepts were confusing to students?
- How well did I summarize the key points at the end of the lecture?
- How well did the lecture prepare students for upcoming assignments or exams?
- How well did I manage time?

There are several advantages of journaling. First, we are more likely to approach the reflection process in a thoughtful, comprehensive way when we write rather than just think about our teaching. Second, making changes to our teaching practices may be more likely when we keep a journal. The journal becomes a resource we can refer to and use prior to delivering the same lecture next semester. As several months may pass before using that specific lecture again, it is easy for us to forget our ideas about how to improve the lecture. Our reflective notes can jog our memory and help us put these ideas into practice. Third, journals can become an excellent way to reflect on our overall growth as educators. Rereading our journal entries can reinforce the changes and improvements that were made. As many institutions incorporate self-assessment into the evaluation or tenure and promotion process, journals may be used to document our growth and provide specific examples of how we have changed our teaching practices to improve student learning.

VIDEO AND AUDIO RECORDINGS

Listening or watching yourself lecture is perhaps one of the best ways to evaluate the effectiveness of your lecture. It is often difficult to watch ourselves teach, but seeing or hearing our own lectures helps illustrate aspects of the lecture that worked well and where improvements might be needed. Research has shown that videotaping can lead to improved lecture performance (Hendricson, 1983). Kpanja (2001) assessed student teacher performance, comparing student teachers who had access to videotapes to those who did not. Results of this study indicated that confidence and performance improved when students were able to review videotapes of their teaching. Although recordings are widely used as a learning tool in undergraduate and graduate education, this is often not the case in the professional world. This is unfortunate because much can be learned when we watch or listen to our lectures, and we should encourage the use of these powerful tools in higher education.

Readily available and inexpensive technology tools, such as mobile devices, make it fairly simple to record lectures by using their built-in cameras and recording tools. Audio recordings are obviously easier to use, especially if you move around the classroom, but video recordings can give you more data about your lecturing style as well as student engagement during your lecture. Bergman (2015) found that audio and video recordings were both beneficial, but video recordings provided valuable information on student nonverbal communication and teacher movement around the room. In addition to providing an evaluative tool that can guide in planning future lectures, the recordings could also be posted online for students who may benefit from hearing the content more than once. Thus, recording lectures can have several advantages.

As you listen to the audio recording or watch the video recording, you can use a broad perspective or take a more specific, targeted approach. Faculty who listen or watch the recordings from a broad perspective often focus on the overall quality of the lecture, asking themselves questions such as, “Did I clearly explain the concepts?” or “Was my lecture well organized and informative?" In other words, the focus is on a general impression of the effectiveness of the lecture. Another approach is to be more targeted in reviewing the recordings, focusing on just one or two elements of the lecture. For instance, perhaps you have been working on activating prior knowledge in a more explicit way. If this is the case, listen or view the recordings from this lens, only focusing on the strategies you used to activate prior knowledge. As you review the recording, document when and how you explicitly activated prior knowledge for your students. In addition, identify missed opportunities when you didn't activate prior knowledge, but you believe it could have been helpful to do so. Given the time constraints we are faced with as professors, it is not likely that we will have the time to review every recording in a thorough manner. However, having the recordings available can allow us to incorporate the data into our assessment practices as needed. It's not necessary to spend hours reviewing every lecture. However, periodically reviewing recordings, especially when we are trying to incorporate a new technique into the lecture, can be a very powerful way to improve our lecturing skills.

To further take advantage of this powerful learning tool, we can review the recordings of our teaching with a faculty colleague or instructional designer from the campus faculty development center. Ozcakar and colleagues (2009) found that reviewing videotapes with an evaluator was more likely to lead to improved performance compared to receiving feedback from the evaluator without the visual component. Thus, combining self-assessment and peer assessment using videotapes of our performance might lead to the best outcomes.

STUDENT ENGAGEMENT AND INTERACTIVITY DATA

Learning is most likely to occur when students are cognitively engaged (Mayer, 2009). Therefore, feedback about student engagement can be meaningful to you as you assess the effectiveness of your lecture. One simple, yet informal, way to assess student engagement is to look at the nonverbal communication patterns in the class. Many of us do this naturally during class, often making slight changes to our lectures when students seem to be losing focus or exhibit low levels of engagement.

A more formal approach that can be used during class is to ask students to self-report their level of engagement at various points of the lecture. An online polling tool can be used for this purpose so students can respond anonymously and you can have easy access to class-level data. Although these data could be immediately useful during class, they can also be used to evaluate patterns of high- and low-level engagement. We can then use this information as we prepare even more effective lectures. For example, we might notice that engagement is lower for certain topics or after prolonged lecturing without an opportunity for reflection. Thus, we will want to use different, more meaningful examples; more explicitly make the concepts more relevant; or incorporate a brief activity. Even this action of asking students to self-evaluate their engagement may result in increased attention and engagement.

An interactivity chart is another tool that can be used to gather student engagement data. To use this tool, print a seating chart and then use it to illustrate when students are interacting with you or their classmates (Acheson, 1981). For instance, you could draw an arrow from the person talking to the person responding. This works best for whole-class discussions because it can be challenging to capture the interactivity patterns when students are working in small groups. As this is a difficult task to do while class discussions are occurring, it is typically helpful to record the class and then fill out the interactivity chart while watching the recording of the class session. If you like the idea of the interactivity chart but worry that you may not have the time after class to review the recording, consider asking a colleague to come into your class to complete the activity chart during the live class session. Although interactivity patterns only show verbal interactions and can't assess cognitive engagement, this tool can show you which students are most actively involved in conversations. Some professors who have used this technique are surprised when they see with whom they interact most frequently or which students are not actively engaged even during active learning breaks from the lecture. It may also be a way for faculty to determine if they are unintentionally interacting more with some groups of students than others (e.g., males versus females). We do need to exercise caution, though, when interpreting these data because a student who fails to ask questions or verbally interact with classmates may still be very cognitively engaged.

STUDENT SURVEYS

Asking students to complete surveys about the lecture is another way to obtain useful data by using questions that target the lecture content and delivery. Using objective survey questions makes it easy to administer and then review class results. Surveys can be administered after every lecture, periodically throughout the semester, or strategically when using a new lecture enhancement technique. A sample lecture survey is provided in Figure 11.1.

Figure 11.1. Lecture survey.

Lecture Survey
Your feedback about today's lecture is very important. Please take a few minutes to complete this anonymous survey about your experience in the lecture. This information will help me improve future lectures. Thank you in advance for your time and feedback.
1. Did assignments help prepare you for the lecture? Not really To some degree Definitely
2. What best describes the level of difficulty regarding the lecture content? Too easy Just right Too difficult
3. Did the examples assist you with understanding the content? Not really To some degree Definitely
4. Were you able to determine which topics were most important? Not really To some degree Definitely
5. Did the reflection exercises help you better understand the content? Not really To some degree Definitely
6. Did the questions help you think more deeply about the content? Not really To some degree Definitely
7. What major point(s) did you take away, or learn, from the lecture today?

Surveys can also include open-ended questions, giving students the opportunity to elaborate on their experiences in the lecture. Although it can be more time consuming to collect and review data from open-ended questions, professors typically find this type of feedback particularly meaningful. Research has shown that when faculty gather and reflect on student survey data about the lectures, the quality of future lectures improves. For example, Winchester and Winchester (2014), found a positive relationship between faculty reflection and teaching effectiveness; faculty who participated in higher levels of reflection had more positive student evaluations.

STUDENT PERFORMANCE DATA

Although many variables influence student learning, the effectiveness of our lectures is one important factor. We can't judge our lectures solely on student performance; however, how well our students do on quizzes, exams, or other academic activities connected to our lecture content does provide us with some insight on the effectiveness of our lectures. For example, if most students didn't perform well on one section of the exam, we may want to think about how much time we devoted to that section during our lecture and if the lecturing strategies we used could be improved. On the other hand, if students performed particularly well on a section of an exam, we would also want to reflect on how we addressed this content in our lecture, because their high-level performance provides some evidence that this approach was successful. Analyzing student performance on a more specific level will provide us with more meaningful data as opposed to reviewing overall scores. For example, let's assume the average grade on an exam is a C. How could we use this information to improve our teaching practices? We don't know if performance for all content areas hovered in the C range or if students did exceptionally well on some topics and really struggled with others, averaging to the C grade. In other words, knowing the average final exam score doesn't provide us with much guidance on how to make improvements. By closely looking at individual questions and identifying sections or topics and analyzing student performance in this way, we may discover that students really seemed to master some content and had difficulty learning other content. We can take this type of student performance feedback and compare it to our lecture to look at how much time we devoted to each of the topics, the examples or activities we used, and whether we incorporated opportunities for retrieval practice. It is likely we will discover several places where improvements to our lecture could be made. It is possible students struggled because of factors not related to the effectiveness of our lecture. Perhaps some concepts required more practice than others, and students didn't exert high levels of effort and time for those concepts. It could also be that students performed better on one of our exams than another because their other academic obligations were different. This is often the case during midterms and finals when students have to divide their study time and efforts across many courses. Because there are so many variables that have an impact on student performance, it is important to exercise caution as we use student performance data to better understand the effectiveness of our lectures, perhaps not rushing to make changes based solely on these data. Nonetheless, high student performance is the goal and should be one factor we consider as we assess our teaching.

FACULTY LEARNING COMMUNITIES

Although specific purposes of faculty learning communities vary, the overarching goal is to improve teaching and learning through instilling a sense of community and structured scholarly discussions. Cox (2004) defined a *learning community* as a group of faculty and staff who "engage in an active, collaborative, yearlong program with a curriculum about enhancing teaching and learning and with frequent seminars and activities that provide learning, development, the scholarship of teaching, and community building" (p. 8).

Research over the past 20 years has consistently shown that faculty learning communities have a positive impact on teaching and learning (Cox, 2004; Smith et al., 2008). Teaching and learning centers could host a topical faculty learning community where a small group of faculty work together over the course of the semester with a specific goal of improving lectures or incorporating quick engagement techniques into classes that have been primarily lecture based. The purpose of this community would be for colleagues to provide honest and constructive feedback to one another about lecturing techniques in a supportive environment. A group of faculty that trusts and respects one another will make meaningful feedback much more likely. Thus, many faculty learning communities focus on building rapport and respect among the participating members during the first few weeks. During this time, faculty members typically share their goals for participation and get to know one another. The second phase often focuses on scholarly research on teaching and learning with discussions about what constitutes effective lecturing or the integration of lecturing with quick, engaged learning techniques. In many cases, books or other resources are shared, reviewed, and discussed by members. Faculty members who participate in these discussions often feel better equipped to provide meaningful feedback to colleagues. Discussions focused on building a research-based understanding of the pedagogy of lectures will serve members well as they shift to the feedback phase.

The heart of this approach lies in the feedback faculty members provide to one another that is aimed at helping one another improve their lecturing technique. Among the variety of approaches that can be used for this purpose, the reflection and discussion approach relies on each participant taking turns and sharing reflections and self-assessments of his or her lecture. The role of the other members is to listen and ask questions that encourage the participant to more deeply reflect on the effectiveness of his or her lecture. In another approach, observing and then sharing feedback, faculty members visit the classes of their colleagues prior to the discussion. This can be done very informally with observations and constructive suggestions shared verbally at the next meeting or more formally with written peer observations (discussed in the next section). Including a visitation component may not always be feasible because of similar teaching schedules or other commitments. If this is the case, participants can share an audio or video tape of the lecture prior to or even during the meeting. Although all types of feedback can be helpful, feedback based on live observations or recorded lectures will obviously be much more specific and meaningful than feedback based on a summary or description of what happened.

Faculty learning communities can also convene in an online setting. Cowie (1997) argued that collaborating with professional peers electronically has advantages over in-person dialogues. For instance, the online component requires writing instead of speaking, and writing can often promote higher levels of reflection. In addition, Cowie discussed how colleagues have the opportunity to think and reflect before responding when engaged in written versus verbal communication. Research has shown that students engage in higher levels of critical thinking when taking part in online discussions as opposed to in-person discussions (Guiller, Durndell, & Ross, 2008). It makes sense that this would also be true for faculty conversations. Increased participation is also more likely because of the flexibility offered through asynchronous learning communities. An additional advantage of online forums for faculty learning communities is that faculty peers from other institutions can participate. Faculty may be more comfortable putting themselves in a vulnerable position and being very open about their teaching successes and failures when working with peers from other institutions who are not involved in tenure and promotion decisions.

Research has also found that reflective practice programming is beneficial (Daniels, Pirayoff, & Bessant, 2013). Hubball, Collins, and Pratt (2005), found that faculty who participated in learning communities addressing reflective practice more deeply explored their teaching beliefs and actions compared to faculty who did not participate in this type of faculty development programming. Taking time out to explore the effectiveness of our teaching approaches in a collaborative, supportive community can therefore lead to positive outcomes.

PEER OBSERVATION

Many teaching and learning centers offer faculty the opportunity to participate in the peer observation process. In some cases, this involves a mentor or member of the teaching and learning center staff conducting a classroom observation. In another case, the center may offer a program for faculty to learn how to conduct peer observations and then work with another faculty member and participate in reciprocal peer observations. With both approaches, the purpose is to improve the teaching and learning process. Peer observations are typically voluntary and confidential and are not connected to formal tenure and promotion processes. A peer observation can be an incredibly helpful tool for faculty interested in assessing and improving their lectures (Sullivan, Buckle, Nicky, & Atkinson, 2012). Research has shown that faculty benefit not only from the feedback received from the observer but also from the experience of being an observer (Hendry & Oliver, 2012; Kohut, Burnap, & Yon, 2007).

The peer observation process typically involves three steps. The first step is for the faculty member and peer observer to meet to discuss the lecture. During this preobservation meeting, the purpose of the observation and issues related to confidentiality are discussed. In addition, the peer observer learns about the overall course learning outcomes, how this lecture fits into the context of the course goals, related activities or assignments leading up to the lecture, and the plan for the lecture. Planning documents could be provided, or the plan could be discussed more generally. The faculty member being observed may also want to identify specific components of the lecture that he or she would like targeted feedback on. For example, if the faculty member wants specific feedback about engagement, they might discuss whether an interactivity chart would be helpful. This is also the time to address the logistics of the observation, such as where the observer should sit and the type of introduction, if any, that will be made to the students. The format and content of the observation report should also be discussed. By the end of this meeting, the observer should have a clear picture of the class, and both parties should be clear on the goals of the observation.

The second step is the actual observation. During the classroom visit, the peer observer brings a laptop, tablet, or notebook and records a time line, summary, and observations of the lecture. Faculty often find it very helpful to see how much time was actually spent on different topics or activities. Observers will find that capturing details in the summary and notes makes writing the classroom observation report a much easier task. After the class is over, the peer colleague documents the observation in a written report.

The third step of the process is the postobservation meeting, which typically begins with the faculty member sharing her or his own self-assessment of the lecture. Next, the observer provides feedback, being sure to address any predesignated target areas. Providing faculty with specific feedback highlighting the effective components of the lecture and constructive feedback that could possibly improve the lecture is beneficial. Faculty can continue to reflect on this experience after the postobservation meeting and, in some cases, may even want to request a follow-up meeting for further discussion.

CLASSROOM OBSERVATION FORM

It is unfortunate that faculty who lecture sometimes feel pressured to move away from this teaching method to obtain positive teaching evaluations. This stems from the national push for active learning that has resulted in the lecture being viewed as an inferior teaching method. It is hoped that the research discussed throughout this book will help us shift to a more positive mind-set about the lecture and a recognition of the many different formats of lecturing. The lecture most certainly still has a place in higher education. Instead of abandoning an effective teaching method, let's focus on how to increase learning and engagement using the lecture.

Most colleges and universities use generic classroom observation forms regardless of the teaching method used. Many forms even favor active learning teaching methods over the lecture and may not address key elements of effective lectures. The form in Figure 11.2 has been designed to evaluate professors who focus more time on the lecture. Questions targeting the lecture can help evaluators provide more specific feedback about the lecturing technique, which will in turn set the stage for productive conversations about how to enhance and improve the most widely used teaching method.

A primary requirement of the educational experience is for faculty to determine to what extent students have learned during the course and how what they learned can be applied. This is accomplished through examinations, papers, reflective journals, small-group discussions, and a host of other mechanisms. The same should be true of our work as faculty.

Figure 11.2. Classroom observation for lectures.

Faculty member name and department	
Class observed (course code and name)	
Date	
Name and position of observer	
Number of students enrolled and/or present	

Syllabus

1. Organized, clear explanation of learning goals, activities, assignments, and schedule
2. Language and tone that is respectful, positive, and motivational
3. Includes essential information about the course, professor, assignments/grading, and policies

Brief Summary of Premeeting

1. Explanation of how the lesson fits into overall course learning outcomes
2. Learning objectives and main topics for the class that will be observed
3. Assignments or other learning activities previously conducted that relate to the lesson
4. Targeted areas for feedback

Lecture Format

1. Type of lecture (e.g., paper reading, storytelling, discussion based, visually enhanced, demonstration, online, interactive lecture)
2. Appropriateness of lecture format to learning goals (building foundational knowledge, facilitating critical thinking and other important skills)
3. Appropriateness and continuity of engaged learning activities used to complement the lecture (engagement strategies reinforced or allowed for application of the lecture content)

Summary of the Observed Class

1. Time line, sequence, and description of teaching and learning activities

Content Expertise
(Note this section is completed only if observer has expertise in the discipline)

1. Clear explanations of concepts
2. References to scholarly sources
3. Use of relevant and meaningful examples
4. Explicit connections between previously learned and new concepts

Organization and Clarity

1. Shared logical organizational structure for the class with students
2. Maintained sequence and scope appropriate to the course and lesson goals
3. Clearly identified and emphasized most important concepts
4. Regularly conducted comprehension checks before moving on to new content
5. Provided students with opportunity to ask questions and provided clear responses

Effective Integration of Lecture Enhancement Strategies

1. Activated prior knowledge at the start of the class and as appropriate throughout the class
2. Used effective hooks to get and maintain student attention throughout the lecture
3. Used techniques to assist students with differentiating the important from the less important content
4. Provided numerous real-world, meaningful examples
5. Engaged students in reflection activities throughout the lecture and at the conclusion of the class
6. Provided students with opportunities to practice retrieving information previously learned
7. Incorporated questions that promote critical thinking

Technology and Other Resources

1. Incorporated the use of technology into the lecture in a meaningful way
2. Applied research-based multimedia principles when developing and using technology tools such as PowerPoint

Student Engagement and Classroom Management 1. Students' level of attention (on-task behaviors, off-task behaviors were addressed if needed) 2. Student engagement (cognitive and social engagement, opportunities for reflection and interaction as appropriate)
Highlights Specific examples of what worked best

Suggestions
Specific examples of how the lecture could be enhanced

Summary of Postobservation Meeting

1. Faculty member self-assessment and response to evaluation
2. If appropriate, develop a plan to share the implementation of excellent teaching strategies with colleagues
3. Identification of instructional goals and plan (including professional development opportunities) to improve teaching

By the end of each semester we should be able to determine to what extent we were able to build an effective learning environment for our students. Evaluation and reflection are critical aspects of growth for our students and for ourselves.

SUMMARY

It is important to regularly engage in self-reflection to determine to what extent our lecture has been effective and ways it may be improved. Having a growth mind-set should not be encouraged only for our students. Engaging in reflection will help us become better teachers and ultimately improve student learning.

REFERENCES

Acheson, K. A. (1981). *Classroom observation techniques* (IDEA Paper No. 4). Retrieved from ERIC database. (ED202259)

Bergman, D. (2015). Comparing the effects of classroom audio-recording and video-recording on preservice teachers' reflection of practice. *Teacher Educator, 50*, 127–144.

Cowie, N. J. (1997). Collaborative journaling by email: Using the structure of cooperative development to become a more reflective teacher. *Saitama University Review, 33*, 199–210.

Cox, M. D. (2004). Introduction to faculty learning communities. *New Directions for Teaching and Learning, 97*, 5–23.

Daniels, E., Pirayoff, R., & Bessant, S. (2013). Using peer observation and collaboration to improve teaching practices. *Universal Journal of Educational Research, 1*, 268–274.

Guiller, J., Durndell, A., & Ross, A. (2008). Peer interaction and critical thinking: Face-to-face or online discussion? *Learning and Instruction, 18*, 187–200.

Hendricson, W. D. (1983). Effects of providing feedback to lecturers via videotape recordings and observer critiques. *American Journal of Pharmaceutical Education, 47*, 239–244.

Hendry, G. D., & Oliver, G. R. (2012). Seeing is believing: The benefits of peer observation. *Journal of University Teaching and Learning Practice, 9*(1), 1–9.

Hubball, H., Collins, J., & Pratt, D. (2005). Enhancing reflective teaching practices: Implications for faculty development programs. *Canadian Journal of Higher Education, 35*(3), 57–81.

Kohut, G. F., Burnap, C., & Yon, M. G. (2007). Peer observation of teaching: Perceptions of the observer and the observed. *College Teaching, 55*, 19–25.

Kpanja, E. (2001). A study of the effects of video tape recording in microteaching training. *British Journal of Educational Technology, 32*, 483–486. doi:10.1111/1467-8535.00215

Mayer, R. E. (2009) *Multi-media learning* (2nd. ed.). New York, NY: Cambridge University Press.

Ozcakar, N., Mevsim, V., Guldal, D., Gunvar, T., Yildirim, E., Sisli, Z., & Semin, I. (2009). Is the use of videotape recording superior to verbal feedback alone in the teaching of clinical skills? *BMC Public Health*, *9*. doi:10.1186/1471-2458-9-474

Smith, T. R., McGowan, J., Allen, A. R., Johnson, W. I., Dickson, L. J., Najee-ullah, M. A., & Peters, M. (2008). Evaluating the impact of a faculty learning community on STEM teaching and learning. *Journal of Negro Education*, *77*, 203–226.

Sullivan, P. B., Buckle, A., Nicky, G., & Atkinson, S. H. (2012). Peer observation of teaching as a faculty development tool. *BMC Medical Education*, *12*. doi:10.1186/1472-6920-12-26

Titus, P. A., & Gremler, D. D. (2010). Guiding reflective practice: An auditing framework to assess teaching philosophy and style. *Journal of Marketing Education*, *32*, 182–196.

Winchester, T. M., & Winchester, M. K. (2014). A longitudinal investigation of the impact of faculty reflective practices on students' evaluations of teaching. *British Journal of Educational Technology*, *45*, 112–124. doi:10.1111/bjet.12019

Zhao, M. (2012). Teachers' professional development from the perspective of teaching reflection levels. *Chinese Education & Society*, *45*(4), 56–67.

AUTHORS

Christine Harrington is executive director of the New Jersey Center for Student Success at the New Jersey Council of County Colleges. Prior to holding this position, Harrington was a professor of psychology at Middlesex County College where she also served as the director of the Center for the Enrichment of Learning and Teaching for five years. She is the author of a research-based textbook for first-year seminars, *Student Success in College: Doing What Works!* (Cengage Learning, 2016). She also was a contributing author for "The Process of Becoming a Critical Thinker" in *Foundations for Critical Thinking* (National Resource Center for the First-Year Experience and Students in Transition, 2015). She also wrote the following articles in *E-Source for College Transitions*, a peer-reviewed online journal: "Dynamic Lecturing in First-Year Courses: Continuing a Proven Tradition" (Vol. 12, pp. 8–10, 2014) and "Using Peer-Reviewed Research to Teach Academic Study Skills in First-Year Seminars" (Vol. 9, pp. 15–17, 2011). Harrington is currently a reviewer for the *Teaching of Psychology* journal, a publication of the American Psychological Association. She previously served on the editorial board for the *Journal of College Counseling* from 2002 to 2008.

Harrington has been invited to give plenary speeches at national teaching and learning conferences such as the Lilly Conference on College and University Teaching and Learning and at the Annual Conference on the First-Year Experience. She has also been an invited keynote speaker at many colleges and universities across the United States on topics such as lecturing, active learning, motivation, critical thinking, and the syllabus.

Todd Zakrajsek is an associate professor in the Department of Family Medicine at the University of North Carolina at Chapel Hill and an adjunct associate professor for faculty development in the Department of Clinical Sciences at North Carolina State University. Prior to his work in the School of Medicine, he was executive director of the Center for Faculty Excellence at the University of North Carolina at Chapel Hill.

Before arriving at University of North Carolina, Zakrajsek was the inaugural director of the Faculty Center for Innovative Teaching at Central Michigan the University and the founding director of the Center for Teaching and Learning at Southern Oregon University, where he also taught in the psychology department as a tenured associate professor.

Zakrajsek currently directs five Lilly Conferences on College and University Teaching and Learning and has served on numerous educationally related boards, including Lenovo, in partnership with Intel and Microsoft, Education Research Initiative and Microsoft Technology Enriched Instruction Workshops. He holds positions on editorial boards for several journals and has published and presented widely on the topic of student learning, including workshops and conference keynote addresses in 47 states and 11 countries. He is coauthor with Terry Doyle of *The New Science of Learning: How to Learn in Harmony With Your Brain* (Stylus, 2013) and coauthor with Claire Howell Major and Michael S. Harris of *Teaching for Learning: 101 Intentionally-Designed Activities to Put Students on the Path to Success* (Routledge, 2016).

INDEX

Also in The Excellent Teacher series

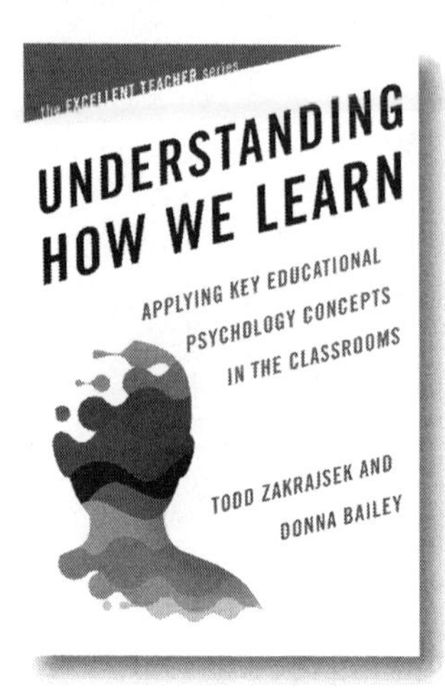

Understanding How We Learn
Applying Key Educational Psychology Concepts in the Classroom

Todd Zakrajsek and Donna Bailey

This succinct, jargon-free, and user-friendly volume offers faculty an introduction to 35 concepts from educational psychology that illuminate what's going through the minds of learners as they grapple with new information.

The concepts are conveniently grouped under major topics, each introduced by a summary of the field, its origins, the latest relevant research, and the implications for teaching: cognition and thinking, memory, learning, perceiving and living in the world, working in groups, motivation, and perceptions of self.

Within each section, Todd Zakrajsek and Donna Bailey provide summaries of each key concept. They explain the terminology, its background, and its relevance to student learning as well as offer ideas and tips for immediate application in teaching.

As an example, the entry on *cognitive load*—the amount of information that the brain can process at any given time and beyond which further input becomes hard to process and usually induces errors—explains its constituent elements, intrinsic, extraneous, and germane, and how they are triggered. The authors conclude with specific tips to reduce cognitive load and strategies to help students encountering difficulties with complex new material understand and accept the need to budget energy and time for certain tasks.

This is an illuminating book for teachers seeking to understand student learning, offering a foundational understanding of educational terms often tossed about in discussions of student learning, and a range of solutions to challenges they commonly encounter in the classroom.